HUNGER OF MEMORY

AN AUTOBIOGRAPHY

Hunger of Memory

THE EDUCATION OF RICHARD RODRIGUEZ

DAVID R. GODINE / PUBLISHER / BOSTON

First published in 1982 by
David R. Godine, Publisher, Inc.
306 Dartmouth Street
Boston, Massachusetts 02116

Library of Congress Cataloging in Publication Data

Rodriguez, Richard
   Hunger of memory.

   1. English language—Acquisition. 2. Bilingualism.
3. Rodriguez, Richard. 4. Mexican Americans—
California—Biography. 5. California—Biography
I. Title.
PE 1066.R65   420'.4261   81-81810
ISBN 0-87923-418-0   AACR2

Fifth printing, December 1982

She tells people, her neighbors, that I am a 'Ph.D. professor.' I am doing some writing, she explains. But I will be going back to teach in a year or two. Soon. In private, she admits worry. 'Did somebody hurt you at Berkeley? ... Why don't you try teaching at some Catholic college?' No, I say. And she turns silent to my father, who stands watching me. The two of them. They know I have money enough to support myself. But I have nothing steady. No profession. And I am the one in the family with so much education. (All those years!) My brother and sisters are doing so well. 'All I want for you is something you can count on for life,' she says.

For her and for him – to honor them.

Middle-class Pastoral

I have taken Caliban's advice. I have stolen their books. I will have some run of this isle.

Once upon a time, I was a 'socially disadvantaged' child. An enchantedly happy child. Mine was a childhood of intense family closeness. And extreme public alienation.

Thirty years later I write this book as a middle-class American man. Assimilated.

Dark-skinned. To be seen at a Belgravia dinner party. Or in New York. Exotic in a tuxedo. My face is drawn to severe Indian features which would pass notice on the page of a *National Geographic*, but at a cocktail party in Bel Air somebody wonders: 'Have you ever thought of doing any high-fashion modeling? Take this card.' (In Beverly Hills will this monster make a man.)

A lady in a green dress asks, 'Didn't we meet at the Thompsons' party last month in Malibu?'

And, 'What do you do, Mr. Rodriguez?'

I write: I am a writer.

A part-time writer. When I began this book, five years ago, a fellowship bought me a year of continuous silence in my San Francisco apartment. But the words wouldn't come. The money ran out. So I was forced to take temporary jobs. (I have friends who, with a phone call, can find me well-paying work.) In past months I have found myself in New York. In Los Angeles. Working. With money. Among people with money. And at leisure – a weekend guest in Connecticut; at a cocktail party in Bel Air.

Perhaps because I have always, accidentally, been a classmate to children of rich parents, I long ago came to assume my association with their world; came to assume that I could have money, if it was money I wanted. But money, big money, has never been the goal of my life. My story is not a version of Sammy Glick's. I work to support my habit of writing. The great luxury of my life is the freedom to sit at this desk.

'Mr.? . . .'

Rodriguez. The name on the door. The name on my passport. The name I carry from my parents – who are no longer my parents, in a cultural sense. This is how I pronounce it: *Rich-heard Road-ree-guess*. This is how I hear it most often.

The voice through a microphone says, 'Ladies and gentlemen, it is with pleasure that I introduce Mr. Richard Rodriguez.'

I am invited very often these days to speak about modern education in college auditoriums and in Holiday Inn ballrooms. I go, still feel a calling to act the teacher, though not licensed by the degree. One time my audience is a convention of university administrators; another time high school teachers of English; another time a women's alumnae group.

'Mr. Rodriguez has written extensively about contemporary education.'

Several essays. I have argued particularly against two government programs – affirmative action and bilingual education.

'He is a provocative speaker.'

I have become notorious among certain leaders of America's Ethnic Left. I am considered a dupe, an ass, the fool – Tom Brown, the brown Uncle Tom, interpreting the writing on the wall to a bunch of cigar-smoking pharaohs.

A dainty white lady at the women's club luncheon approaches the podium after my speech to say, after all, wasn't it a shame that I wasn't able to 'use' my Spanish in school. What a shame. But how dare her lady-fingered pieties extend to my life!

There are those in White America who would anoint me to play out for them some drama of ancestral reconciliation. Perhaps because I am marked by indelible color they easily suppose that I am unchanged by social mobility, that I can claim unbroken ties with my past. The possibility! At a time when many middle-class children and parents grow distant, apart, no longer speak, romantic solutions appeal.

But I reject the role. (Caliban won't ferry a TV crew back to his island, there to recover his roots.)

Aztec ruins hold no special interest for me. I do not search Mexican graveyards for ties to unnamable ancestors. I assume I retain certain features of gesture and mood derived from buried lives. I also speak Spanish today. And read García Lorca and García Márquez at my leisure. But what consolation can that fact bring against the knowledge that my mother and father have never heard of García Lorca or García Márquez? What preoccupies me is immediate: the separation I endure with my parents in loss. This is what matters to me: the story of the scholarship boy who returns home one summer from college to discover bewildering silence, facing his parents. This my story. An American story.

Consider me, if you choose, a comic victim of two cultures. This is my situation: writing these pages, surrounded in the room I am in by volumes of Montaigne and Shakespeare and Lawrence. They are mine now.

A Mexican woman passes in a black dress. She wears a white apron; she carries a tray of hors d'oeuvres. She must only be asking if there are any I want as she proffers the tray like a wheel of good fortune. I shake my head. No. Does she wonder how I am here? In Bel Air.

It is education that has altered my life. Carried me far.

I write this autobiography as the history of my schooling. To admit the change in my life I must speak of years as a student, of losses, of gains.

I consider my book a kind of pastoral. I write in the tradition of that high, courtly genre. But I am no upper-class pastoral singer. Upper-class pastoral can admit envy for the intimate pleasures of rustic life as an arrogant way of reminding its listeners of their difference – their own public power and civic position. ('Let's be shepherds . . . Ah, if only we could.') Unlike the upper class, the middle class lives in a public world, lacking great individual power and standing. Middle-class pastoral is, therefore, a more difficult hymn. There is no grand compensation to the admission of envy of the poor. The middle class rather is tempted by the pastoral impulse to deny its difference from the lower class – even to attempt cheap imitations of lower-class life. ('But I still *am* a shepherd!')

I must resist being tempted by this decadent solution to mass public life. It seems to me dangerous, because in trying to imitate the lower class, the middle class blurs the distinction so crucial to social reform. One can no longer easily say what exactly distinguishes the alien poor.

I do not write as a modern-day Wordsworth seeking to imitate the intimate speech of the poor. I sing Ariel's song to celebrate the intimate speech my family once freely exchanged. In singing the praise of my lower-class past, I remind myself of my separation from that past, bring memory to silence. I turn to consider the boy I once was in order, finally, to describe the man I am now. I remember what was so grievously lost to define what was necessarily gained.

But the New York editor is on the phone and he can't understand: 'Why do you spend so much time on abstract issues? Nobody's going to remember affirmative action in another twenty-five years. The strength of this manuscript is in the narrative. You should write your book in stories – not as a series of essays. Let's have more Grandma.'

But no. Here is my most real life. My book is necessarily political, in the conventional sense, for public issues – editorials and ballot stubs, petitions and placards, faceless formulations of greater and lesser good by greater and lesser minds – have bisected my life and changed its course. And, in some broad sense, my writing is political because it concerns my movement away from the company of family and into the city. This was my coming of age: I became a man by becoming a public man.

This autobiography, moreover, is a book about language. I write about poetry; the new Roman Catholic liturgy; learning to read; writing; political terminology. Language has been the great subject of my life. In college and graduate school, I was registered as an 'English major.' But well before then, from my first day of school, I was a student of language. Obsessed by the way it determined my public identity. The way it permits me here to describe myself, writing . . .

Writing this manuscript. Essays impersonating an autobiography; six chapters of sad, fuguelike repetition.

Now it exists – a weight in my hand. Let the bookstore clerk puzzle over where it should be placed. (Rodriguez? Rodriguez?) Probably he will shelve it alongside specimens of that exotic new genre, 'ethnic literature.' Mistaken, the gullible reader will – in sympathy or in anger – take it that I intend to model my life as the typical Hispanic-American life.

But I write of one life only. My own. If my story is true, I trust it will resonate with significance for other lives. Finally, my history deserves public notice as no more than this: a parable for the life of its reader. Here is the life of a middle-class man.

ONE

Aria

I remember to start with that day in Sacramento – a California now nearly thirty years past – when I first entered a classroom, able to understand some fifty stray English words. The third of four children, I had been preceded to a neighborhood Roman Catholic school by an older brother and sister. But neither of them had revealed very much about their classroom experiences. Each afternoon they returned, as they left in the morning, always together, speaking in Spanish as they climbed the five steps of the porch. And their mysterious books, wrapped in shopping-bag paper, remained on the table next to the door, closed firmly behind them.

An accident of geography sent me to a school where all my classmates were white, many the children of doctors and lawyers and business executives. All my classmates certainly must have been uneasy on that first day of school – as most children are uneasy – to find themselves apart from their families in the first institution of their lives. But I was astonished.

The nun said, in a friendly but oddly impersonal voice, 'Boys and girls, this is Richard Rodriguez.' (I heard her sound out: *Rich-heard Road-ree-guess.*) It was the first time I had heard anyone name me in English. 'Richard,' the nun repeated more slowly, writing my name down in her black leather book. Quickly I turned to see my mother's face dissolve in a watery blur behind the pebbled glass door.

Many years later there is something called bilingual education – a scheme proposed in the late 1960s by Hispanic-American social activists, later endorsed by a congressional vote. It is a program that seeks to permit non-English-speaking children, many from lower-class homes, to use their family language as the language of school. (Such is the goal its supporters announce.) I hear them and am forced to say no: It is not possible for a child – any child – ever to use his family's language in school. Not to understand this is to misunderstand the public uses of schooling and to trivialize the nature of intimate life – a family's 'language.'

Memory teaches me what I know of these matters; the boy reminds the adult. I was a bilingual child, a certain kind – socially disadvantaged – the son of working-class parents, both Mexican immigrants.

In the early years of my boyhood, my parents coped very well in America. My father had steady work. My mother managed at home. They were nobody's victims. Optimism and ambition led them to a house (our home) many blocks from the Mexican south side of town. We lived among *gringos* and only a block from the biggest, whitest houses. It never occurred to my parents that they couldn't live wherever they chose. Nor was the Sacramento of the fifties bent on teaching them a contrary lesson. My mother and father were more annoyed than intimidated by those two or three neighbors who tried initially to make us unwelcome. ('Keep your brats away from my sidewalk!') But despite all they achieved, perhaps because they had so much to achieve, any deep feeling of ease, the confidence of 'belonging' in public was withheld from them both. They regarded the people at work, the faces in crowds, as very distant from us. They were the others, *los gringos*. That term was interchangeable in their speech with another, even more telling, *los americanos*.

I grew up in a house where the only regular guests were my relations. For one day, enormous families of relatives would visit and there would be so many people that the noise and the bodies would spill out to the backyard and front porch. Then, for weeks, no one came by. (It was usually a salesman who rang the doorbell.) Our house stood apart. A gaudy yellow in a row of white bungalows. We were the people with the noisy dog. The people who raised pigeons and chickens. We were the foreigners on the block. A few neighbors smiled and waved. We waved back. But no one in the family knew the names of the old couple who lived next door; until I was seven years old, I did not know the names of the kids who lived across the street.

In public, my father and mother spoke a hesitant, accented, not always grammatical English. And they would have to strain – their bodies tense – to catch the sense of what was rapidly said by *los gringos*. At home they spoke Spanish. The language of their Mexican past sounded in counterpoint to the English of public society. The words would come quickly, with ease. Conveyed through those sounds was the pleasing, soothing, consoling reminder of being at home.

During those years when I was first conscious of hearing, my mother and father addressed me only in Spanish; in Spanish I learned to reply. By contrast, English (*inglés*), rarely heard in the house, was the language I came to associate with *gringos*. I learned my first words of English overhearing my parents speak to strangers. At five years of age, I knew just enough English for my mother to trust me on errands to stores one block away. No more.

I was a listening child, careful to hear the very different sounds of Spanish and English. Wide-eyed with hearing, I'd listen to sounds more than words. First, there were English (*gringo*) sounds. So many words were still unknown that when the butcher or the lady at the drugstore said something to me, exotic polysyllabic sounds would bloom in the midst of their sentences. Often, the speech of people in public seemed to me very loud, booming with confidence. The man behind the counter would literally ask, 'What can I do for you?' But by being so firm and so clear, the sound of his voice said that he was a *gringo*; he belonged in public society.

I would also hear then the high nasal notes of middle-class American speech. The air stirred with sound. Sometimes, even now, when I have been traveling abroad for several weeks, I will hear what I heard as a boy. In hotel lobbies or airports, in Turkey or Brazil, some Americans will pass, and suddenly I will hear it again – the high sound of American voices. For a few seconds I will hear it with pleasure, for it is now the sound of *my* society – a reminder of home. But inevitably – already on the flight headed for home – the sound fades with repetition. I will be unable to hear it anymore.

When I was a boy, things were different. The accent of *los gringos* was never pleasing nor was it hard to hear. Crowds at Safeway or at bus stops would be noisy with sound. And I would be forced to edge away from the chirping chatter above me.

I was unable to hear my own sounds, but I knew very well that I spoke English poorly. My words could not stretch far enough to form complete thoughts. And the words I did speak I didn't know well enough to make into distinct sounds. (Listeners would usually lower their heads, better to hear what I was trying to say.) But it was one thing for *me* to speak English with difficulty. It was more troubling for me to hear my parents speak in public: their high-whining vowels and guttural consonants; their sentences that got stuck with 'eh' and 'ah' sounds; the confused syntax; the hesitant rhythm of sounds so different from the way *gringos* spoke. I'd notice, moreover, that my parents' voices were softer than those of *gringos* we'd meet.

I am tempted now to say that none of this mattered. In adulthood I am embarrassed by childhood fears. And, in a way, it didn't matter very much that my parents could not speak English with ease. Their linguistic difficulties had no serious consequences. My mother and father made themselves understood at the county hospital clinic and at government offices. And yet, in another way, it mattered very much – it was unsettling to hear my parents struggle with English. Hearing them, I'd grow nervous, my clutching trust in their protection and power weakened.

There were many times like the night at a brightly lit gasoline station (a blaring white memory) when I stood uneasily, hearing my father. He was talking to a teenaged attendant. I do not recall what they were saying, but I cannot forget the sounds my father made as he spoke. At one point his words slid together to form one word – sounds as confused as the threads of blue and green oil in the puddle next to my shoes. His voice rushed through what he had left to say. And, toward the end, reached falsetto notes, appealing to his listener's understanding. I looked away to the lights of passing automobiles. I tried not to hear anymore. But I heard only too well the calm, easy tones in the attendant's reply. Shortly afterward, walking toward home with my father, I shivered when he put his hand on my shoulder. The very first chance that I got, I evaded his grasp and ran on ahead into the dark, skipping with feigned boyish exuberance.

But then there was Spanish. *Español*: my family's language. *Español*: the language that seemed to me a private language. I'd hear strangers on the radio and in the Mexican Catholic church across town speaking in Spanish, but I couldn't really believe that Spanish was a public language, like English. Spanish speakers, rather, seemed related to me, for I sensed that we shared – through our language – the experience of feeling apart from *los gringos*. It was thus a ghetto Spanish that I heard and I spoke. Like those whose lives are bound by a barrio, I was reminded by Spanish of my separateness from *los otros, los gringos* in power. But more intensely than for most barrio children – because I did not live in a barrio – Spanish seemed to me the language of home. (Most days it was only at home that I'd hear it.) It became the language of joyful return.

A family member would say something to me and I would feel myself specially recognized. My parents would say something to me and I would feel embraced by the sounds of their words. Those sounds said: *I am speaking with ease in Spanish. I am addressing you in words I never use with* los gringos. *I recognize you as someone special, close, like no one outside. You belong with us. In the family.*

(*Ricardo.*)

At the age of five, six, well past the time when most other children no longer easily notice the difference between sounds uttered at home and words spoken in public, I had a different experience. I lived in a world magically compounded of sounds. I remained a child longer than most; I lingered too long, poised at the edge of language – often frightened by the sounds of *los gringos*, delighted by the sounds of Spanish at home. I shared with my family a language that was startlingly different from that used in the great city around us.

For me there were none of the gradations between public and private society so normal to a maturing child. Outside the house was public society; inside the house was private. Just opening or closing the screen door behind me was an important experience. I'd rarely leave home all alone or without reluctance. Walking down the sidewalk, under the canopy of tall trees, I'd warily notice the – suddenly – silent neighborhood kids who stood warily watching me. Nervously, I'd arrive at the grocery store to hear there the sounds of the *gringo* – foreign to me – reminding me that in this world so big, I was a foreigner. But then I'd return. Walking back toward our house, climbing the steps from the sidewalk, when the front door was open in summer, I'd hear voices beyond the screen door talking in Spanish. For a second or two, I'd stay, linger there, listening. Smiling, I'd hear my mother call out, saying in Spanish (words): 'Is that you, Richard?' All the while her sounds would assure me: *You are home now; come closer; inside. With us.*

'*Sí,*' I'd reply.

Once more inside the house I would resume (assume) my place in the family. The sounds would dim, grow harder to hear. Once more at home, I would grow less aware of that fact. It required, however, no more than the blurt of the doorbell to alert me to listen to sounds all over again. The house would turn instantly still while my mother went to the door. I'd hear her hard English sounds. I'd wait to hear her voice return to soft-sounding Spanish, which assured me, as surely as did the clicking tongue of the lock on the door, that the stranger was gone.

Plainly, it is not healthy to hear such sounds so often. It is not healthy to distinguish public words from private sounds so easily. I remained cloistered by sounds, timid and shy in public, too dependent on voices at home. And yet it needs to be emphasized: I was an extremely happy child at home. I remember many nights when my father would come back from work, and I'd hear him call out to my mother in Spanish, sounding relieved. In Spanish, he'd sound light and free notes he never could manage in English. Some nights I'd jump up just at hearing his voice. With *mis hermanos* I would come running into the room where he was with my mother. Our laughing (so deep was the pleasure!) became screaming. Like others who know the pain of public alienation, we transformed the knowledge of our public separateness and made it consoling – the reminder of intimacy. Excited, we joined our voices in a celebration of sounds. *We are speaking now the way we never speak out in public. We are alone – together*, voices sounded, surrounded to tell me. Some nights, no one seemed willing to loosen the hold sounds had on us. At dinner, we invented new words. (Ours sounded Spanish, but made sense only to us.) We pieced together new words by taking, say, an English verb and giving it Spanish endings. My mother's instructions at bedtime would be lacquered with mock-urgent tones. Or a word like *sí* would become, in several notes, able to convey added measures of feeling. Tongues explored the edges of words, especially the fat vowels. And we happily sounded that military drum roll, the twirling roar of the Spanish *r*. Family language: my family's sounds. The voices of my parents and sisters and brother. Their voices insisting: *You belong here. We are family members. Related. Special to one another. Listen!* Voices singing and sighing, rising, straining, then surging, teeming with pleasure that burst syllables into fragments of laughter. At times it seemed there was steady quiet only when, from another room, the rustling whispers of my parents faded and I moved closer to sleep.

2

Supporters of bilingual education today imply that students like me miss a great deal by not being taught in their family's language. What they seem not to recognize is that, as a socially disadvantaged child, I considered Spanish to be a private language. What I needed to learn in school was that I had the right – and the obligation – to speak the public language of *los gringos*. The odd truth is that my first-grade classmates could have become bilingual, in the conventional sense of that word, more easily than I. Had they been taught (as upper-middle-class children are often taught early) a second language like Spanish or French, they could have regarded it simply as that: another public language. In my case such bilingualism could not have been so quickly achieved. What I did not believe was that I could speak a single public language.

Without question, it would have pleased me to hear my teachers address me in Spanish when I entered the classroom. I would have felt much less afraid. I would have trusted them and responded with ease. But I would have delayed – for how long postponed? – having to learn the language of public society. I would have evaded – and for how long could I have afforded to delay? – learning the great lesson of school, that I had a public identity.

Fortunately, my teachers were unsentimental about their responsibility. What they understood was that I needed to speak a public language. So their voices would search me out, asking me questions. Each time I'd hear them, I'd look up in surprise to see a nun's face frowning at me. I'd mumble, not really meaning to answer. The nun would persist, 'Richard, stand up. Don't look at the floor. Speak up. Speak to the entire class, not just to me!' But I couldn't believe that the English language was mine to use. (In part, I did not want to believe it.) I continued to mumble. I resisted the teacher's demands. (Did I somehow suspect that once I learned public language my pleasing family life would be changed?) Silent, waiting for the bell to sound, I remained dazed, diffident, afraid.

Because I wrongly imagined that English was intrinsically a public language and Spanish an intrinsically private one, I easily noted the difference between classroom language and the language of home. At school, words were directed to a general audience of listeners. ('Boys and girls.') Words were meaningfully ordered. And the point was not self-expression alone but to make oneself understood by many others. The teacher quizzed: 'Boys and girls, why do we use that word in this sentence? Could we think of a better word to use there? Would the sentence change its meaning if the words were differently arranged? And wasn't there a better way of saying much the same thing?' (I couldn't say. I wouldn't try to say.)

Three months. Five. Half a year passed. Unsmiling, ever watchful, my teachers noted my silence. They began to connect my behavior with the difficult progress my older sister and brother were making. Until one Saturday morning three nuns arrived at the house to talk to our parents. Stiffly, they sat on the blue living room sofa. From the doorway of another room, spying the visitors, I noted the incongruity – the clash of two worlds, the faces and voices of school intruding upon the familiar setting of home. I overheard one voice gently wondering, 'Do your children speak only Spanish at home, Mrs. Rodriguez?' While another voice added, 'That Richard especially seems so timid and shy.'

That Rich-heard!

With great tact the visitors continued, 'Is it possible for you and your husband to encourage your children to practice their English when they are home?' Of course, my parents complied. What would they not do for their children's well-being? And how could they have questioned the Church's authority which those women represented? In an instant, they agreed to give up the language (the sounds) that had revealed and accentuated our family's closeness. The moment after the visitors left, the change was observed. '*Ahora*, speak to us *en inglés*,' my father and mother united to tell us.

At first, it seemed a kind of game. After dinner each night, the family gathered to practice 'our' English. (It was still then *inglés*, a language foreign to us, so we felt drawn as strangers to it.) Laughing, we would try to define words we could not pronounce. We played with strange English sounds, often over-anglicizing our pronunciations. And we filled the smiling gaps of our sentences with familiar Spanish sounds. But that was cheating, somebody shouted. Everyone laughed. In school, meanwhile, like my brother and sister, I was required to attend a daily tutoring session. I needed a full year of special attention. I also needed my teachers to keep my attention from straying in class by calling out, *Rich-heard* – their English voices slowly prying loose my ties to my other name, its three notes, *Ri-car-do*. Most of all I needed to hear my mother and father speak to me in a moment of seriousness in broken – suddenly heartbreaking – English. The scene was inevitable: One Saturday morning I entered the kitchen where my parents were talking in Spanish. I did not realize that they were talking in Spanish however until, at the moment they saw me, I heard their voices change to speak English. Those *gringo* sounds they uttered startled me. Pushed me away. In that moment of trivial misunderstanding and profound insight, I felt my throat twisted by unsounded grief. I turned quickly and left the room. But I had no place to escape to with Spanish. (The spell was broken.) My brother and sisters were speaking English in another part of the house.

Again and again in the days following, increasingly angry, I was obliged to hear my mother and father: 'Speak to us *en inglés.*' (*Speak.*) Only then did I determine to learn classroom English. Weeks after, it happened: One day in school I raised my hand to volunteer an answer. I spoke out in a loud voice. And I did not think it remarkable when the entire class understood. That day, I moved very far from the disadvantaged child I had been only days earlier. The belief, the calming assurance that I belonged in public, had at last taken hold.

Shortly after, I stopped hearing the high and loud sounds of *los gringos*. A more and more confident speaker of English, I didn't trouble to listen to *how* strangers sounded, speaking to me. And there simply were too many English-speaking people in my day for me to hear American accents anymore. Conversations quickened. Listening to persons who sounded eccentrically pitched voices, I usually noted their sounds for an initial few seconds before I concentrated on *what* they were saying. Conversations became content-full. Transparent. Hearing someone's *tone* of voice – angry or questioning or sarcastic or happy or sad – I didn't distinguish it from the words it expressed. Sound and word were thus tightly wedded. At the end of a day, I was often bemused, always relieved, to realize how 'silent,' though crowded with words, my day in public had been. (This public silence measured and quickened the change in my life.)

At last, seven years old, I came to believe what had been technically true since my birth: I was an American citizen.

But the special feeling of closeness at home was diminished by then. Gone was the desperate, urgent, intense feeling of being at home; rare was the experience of feeling myself individualized by family intimates. We remained a loving family, but one greatly changed. No longer so close; no longer bound tight by the pleasing and troubling knowledge of our public separateness. Neither my older brother nor sister rushed home after school anymore. Nor did I. When I arrived home there would often be neighborhood kids in the house. Or the house would be empty of sounds.

Following the dramatic Americanization of their children, even my parents grew more publicly confident. Especially my mother. She learned the names of all the people on our block. And she decided we needed to have a telephone installed in the house. My father continued to use the word *gringo*. But it was no longer charged with the old bitterness or distrust. (Stripped of any emotional content, the word simply became a name for those Americans not of Hispanic descent.) Hearing him, sometimes, I wasn't sure if he was pronouncing the Spanish word *gringo* or saying gringo in English.

Matching the silence I started hearing in public was a new quiet at home. The family's quiet was partly due to the fact that, as we children learned more and more English, we shared fewer and fewer words with our parents. Sentences needed to be spoken slowly when a child addressed his mother or father. (Often the parent wouldn't understand.) The child would need to repeat himself. (Still the parent misunderstood.) The young voice, frustrated, would end up saying, 'Never mind' – the subject was closed. Dinners would be noisy with the clinking of knives and forks against dishes. My mother would smile softly between her remarks; my father at the other end of the table would chew and chew at his food, while he stared over the heads of his children.

My *mother!* My *father!* After English became my primary

language, I no longer knew what words to use in addressing my parents. The old Spanish words (those tender accents of sound) I had used earlier – *mamá* and *papá* – I couldn't use anymore. They would have been too painful reminders of how much had changed in my life. On the other hand, the words I heard neighborhood kids call *their* parents seemed equally unsatisfactory. *Mother* and *Father*; *Ma, Papa, Pa, Dad, Pop* (how I hated the all-American sound of that last word especially) – all these terms I felt were unsuitable, not really terms of address for *my* parents. As a result, I never used them at home. Whenever I'd speak to my parents, I would try to get their attention with eye contact alone. In public conversations, I'd refer to 'my parents' or 'my mother and father.'

My mother and father, for their part, responded differently, as their children spoke to them less. She grew restless, seemed troubled and anxious at the scarcity of words exchanged in the house. It was she who would question me about my day when I came home from school. She smiled at small talk. She pried at the edges of my sentences to get me to say something more. (What?) She'd join conversations she overheard, but her intrusions often stopped her children's talking. By contrast, my father seemed reconciled to the new quiet. Though his English improved somewhat, he retired into silence. At dinner he spoke very little. One night his children and even his wife helplessly giggled at his garbled English pronunciation of the Catholic Grace before Meals. Thereafter he made his wife recite the prayer at the start of each meal, even on formal occasions, when there were guests in the house. Hers became the public voice of the family. On official business, it was she, not my father, one would usually hear on the phone or in stores, talking to strangers. His children grew so accustomed to his silence that, years later, they would speak routinely of his shyness. (My mother would often try to explain: Both his parents died when he was eight. He was raised by an uncle who treated him like little more than a menial servant. He was never encouraged to speak. He grew up alone. A man of few words.) But my father was not shy, I realized, when I'd watch him speaking Spanish with relatives. Using Spanish, he was quickly effusive. Especially when talking with other men, his voice would spark, flicker, flare alive with sounds. In Spanish, he expressed ideas and feelings he rarely revealed in English. With firm Spanish sounds, he conveyed confidence and authority English would never allow him.

The silence at home, however, was finally more than a literal silence. Fewer words passed between parent and child, but more profound was the silence that resulted from my inattention to sounds. At about the time I no longer bothered to listen with care to the sounds of English in public, I grew careless about listening to the sounds family members made when they spoke. Most of the time I heard someone speaking at home and didn't distinguish his sounds from the words people uttered in public. I didn't even pay much attention to my parents' accented and ungrammatical speech. At least not at home. Only when I was with them in public would I grow alert to their accents. Though, even then, their sounds caused me less and less concern. For I was increasingly confident of my own public identity.

I would have been happier about my public success had I not sometimes recalled what it had been like earlier, when my family had conveyed its intimacy through a set of conveniently private sounds. Sometimes in public, hearing a stranger, I'd hark back to my past. A Mexican farmworker approached me downtown to ask directions to somewhere. '¿*Hijito* . . . ?' he said. And his voice summoned deep longing. Another time, standing beside my mother in the visiting room of a Carmelite convent, before the dense screen which rendered the nuns shadowy figures, I heard several Spanish-speaking nuns – their busy, singsong overlapping voices – assure us that yes, yes, we were remembered, all our family was remembered in their prayers. (Their voices echoed faraway family sounds.) Another day, a dark-faced old woman – her hand light on my shoulder – steadied herself against me as she boarded a bus. She murmured something I couldn't quite comprehend. Her Spanish voice came near, like the face of a never-before-seen relative in the instant before I was kissed. Her voice, like so many of the Spanish voices I'd hear in public, recalled the golden age of my youth. Hearing Spanish then, I continued to be a careful, if sad, listener to sounds. Hearing a Spanish-speaking family walking behind me, I turned to look. I smiled for an instant, before my glance found the Hispanic-looking faces of strangers in the crowd going by.

Today I hear bilingual educators say that children lose a degree of 'individuality' by becoming assimilated into public society. (Bilingual schooling was popularized in the seventies, that decade when middle-class ethnics began to resist the process of assimilation – the American melting pot.) But the bilingualists simplistically scorn the value and necessity of assimilation. They do not seem to realize that there are *two* ways a person is individualized. So they do not realize that while one suffers a diminished sense of *private* individuality by becoming assimilated into public society, such assimilation makes possible the achievement of *public* individuality.

The bilingualists insist that a student should be reminded of his difference from others in mass society, his heritage. But they equate mere separateness with individuality. The fact is that only in private – with intimates – is separateness from the crowd a prerequisite for individuality. (An intimate draws me apart, tells me that I am unique, unlike all others.) In public, by contrast, full individuality is achieved, paradoxically, by those who are able to consider themselves members of the crowd. Thus it happened for me: Only when I was able to think of myself as an American, no longer an alien in *gringo* society, could I seek the rights and opportunities necessary for full public individuality. The social and political advantages I enjoy as a man result from the day that I came to believe that my name, indeed, is *Rich-heard Road-ree-guess.* It is true that my public society today is often impersonal. (My public society is usually mass society.) Yet despite the anonymity of the crowd and despite the fact that the individuality I achieve in public is often tenuous – because it depends on my being one in a crowd – I celebrate the day I acquired my new name. Those middle-class ethnics who scorn assimilation seem to me filled with decadent self-pity, obsessed by the burden of public life. Dangerously, they romanticize public separateness and they trivialize the dilemma of the socially disadvantaged.

My awkward childhood does not prove the necessity of bilingual education. My story discloses instead an essential myth of childhood – inevitable pain. If I rehearse here the changes in my private life after my Americanization, it is finally to emphasize the public gain. The loss implies the gain: The house I returned to each afternoon was quiet. Intimate sounds no longer rushed to the door to greet me. There were other noises inside. The telephone rang. Neighborhood kids ran past the door of the bedroom where I was reading my schoolbooks – covered with shopping-bag paper. Once I learned public language, it would never again be easy for me to hear intimate family voices. More and more of my day was spent hearing words. But that may only be a way of saying that the day I raised my hand in class and spoke loudly to an entire roomful of faces, my childhood started to end.

3

I grew up victim to a disabling confusion. As I grew fluent in English, I no longer could speak Spanish with confidence. I continued to understand spoken Spanish. And in high school, I learned how to read and write Spanish. But for many years I could not pronounce it. A powerful guilt blocked my spoken words; an essential glue was missing whenever I'd try to connect words to form sentences. I would be unable to break a barrier of sound, to speak freely. I would speak, or try to speak, Spanish, and I would manage to utter halting, hiccuping sounds that betrayed my unease.

When relatives and Spanish-speaking friends of my parents came to the house, my brother and sisters seemed reticent to use Spanish, but at least they managed to say a few necessary words before being excused. I never managed so gracefully. I was cursed with guilt. Each time I'd hear myself addressed in Spanish, I would be unable to respond with any success. I'd know the words I wanted to say, but I couldn't manage to say them. I would try to speak, but everything I said seemed to me horribly anglicized. My mouth would not form the words right. My jaw would tremble. After a phrase or two, I'd cough up a warm, silvery sound. And stop.

It surprised my listeners to hear me. They'd lower their heads, better to grasp what I was trying to say. They would repeat their questions in gentle, affectionate voices. But by then I would answer in English. No, no, they would say, we want you to speak to us in Spanish. ('. . . *en español.*') But I couldn't do it. *Pocho* then they called me. Sometimes playfully, teasingly, using the tender diminutive – *mi pochito*. Sometimes not so playfully, mockingly, *Pocho*. (A Spanish dictionary defines that word as an adjective meaning 'colorless' or 'bland.' But I heard it as a noun, naming the Mexican-American who, in becoming an American, forgets his native society.) '¡*Pocho*!' the lady in the Mexican food store muttered, shaking her head. I looked up to the counter where red and green peppers were strung like Christmas tree lights and saw the frowning face of the stranger. My mother laughed somewhere behind me. (She said that her children didn't want to practice 'our Spanish' after they started going to school.) My mother's smiling voice made me suspect that the lady who faced me was not really angry at me. But, searching her face, I couldn't find the hint of a smile.

Embarrassed, my parents would regularly need to explain their children's inability to speak flowing Spanish during those years. My mother met the wrath of her brother, her only brother, when he came up from Mexico one summer with his family. He saw his nieces and nephews for the very first time. After listening to me, he looked away and said what a disgrace it was that I couldn't speak Spanish, '*su propio idioma.*' He made that remark to my mother; I noticed, however, that he stared at my father.

I clearly remember one other visitor from those years. A long-time friend of my father from San Francisco would come to stay with us for several days in late August. He took great interest in me after he realized that I couldn't answer his questions in Spanish. He would grab me as I started to leave the kitchen. He would ask me something. Usually he wouldn't bother to wait for my mumbled response. Knowingly, he'd murmur: '¿*Ay Pocho, Pocho, adónde vas?*' And he would press his thumbs into the upper part of my arms, making me squirm with currents of pain. Dumbly, I'd stand there, waiting for his wife to notice us, for her to call him off with a benign smile. I'd giggle, hoping to deflate the tension between us, pretending that I hadn't seen the glittering scorn in his glance.

I remember that man now, but seek no revenge in this telling. I recount such incidents only because they suggest the fierce power Spanish had for many people I met at home; the way Spanish was associated with closeness. Most of those people who called me a *pocho* could have spoken English to me. But they would not. They seemed to think that Spanish was the only language we could use, that Spanish alone permitted our close association. (Such persons are vulnerable always to the ghetto merchant and the politician who have learned the value of speaking their clients' family language to gain immediate trust.) For my part, I felt that I had somehow committed a sin of betrayal by learning English. But betrayal against whom? Not against visitors to the house exactly. No, I felt that I had betrayed my immediate family. I *knew* that my parents had encouraged me to learn English. I *knew* that I had turned to English only with angry reluctance. But once I spoke English with ease, I came to *feel* guilty. (This guilt defied logic.) I felt that I had shattered the intimate bond that had once held the family close. This original sin against my family told whenever anyone addressed me in Spanish and I responded, confounded.

But even during those years of guilt, I was coming to sense

certain consoling truths about language and intimacy. I remember playing with a friend in the backyard one day, when my grandmother appeared at the window. Her face was stern with suspicion when she saw the boy (the *gringo*) I was with. In Spanish she called out to me, sounding the whistle of her ancient breath. My companion looked up and watched her intently as she lowered the window and moved, still visible, behind the light curtain, watching us both. He wanted to know what she had said. I started to tell him, to say – to translate her Spanish words into English. The problem was, however, that though I knew how to translate exactly *what* she had told me, I realized that any translation would distort the deepest meaning of her message: It had been directed only to me. This message of intimacy could never be translated because it was not *in* the words she had used but passed *through* them. So any translation would have seemed wrong; her words would have been stripped of an essential meaning. Finally, I decided not to tell my friend anything. I told him that I didn't hear all she had said.

This insight unfolded in time. Making more and more friends outside my house, I began to distinguish intimate voices speaking through *English*. I'd listen at times to a close friend's confidential tone or secretive whisper. Even more remarkable were those instances when, for no special reason apparently, I'd become conscious of the fact that my companion was speaking only to me. I'd marvel just hearing his voice. It was a stunning event: to be able to break through his words, to be able to hear this voice of the other, to realize that it was directed only to me. After such moments of intimacy outside the house, I began to trust hearing intimacy conveyed through my family's English. Voices at home at last punctured sad confusion. I'd hear myself addressed as an intimate at home once again. Such moments were never as raucous with sound as past times had been when we had had 'private' Spanish to use. (Our English-sounding house was never to be as noisy as our Spanish-speaking house had been.) Intimate moments were usually soft moments of sound. My mother was in the dining room while I did my homework nearby. And she looked over at me. Smiled. Said something – her words said nothing very important. But her voice sounded to tell me (*We are together*) I was her son.

(*Richard!*)

Intimacy thus continued at home; intimacy was not stilled by English. It is true that I would never forget the great change of my life, the diminished occasions of intimacy. But there would also be times when I sensed the deepest truth about language and intimacy: *Intimacy is not created by a particular language; it is created by intimates.* The great change in my life was not linguistic but social. If, after becoming a successful student, I no longer heard intimate voices as often as I had earlier, it was not because I spoke English rather than Spanish. It was because I used public language for most of the day. I moved easily at last, a citizen in a crowded city of words.

4

This boy became a man. In private now, alone, I brood over language and intimacy – the great themes of my past. In public I expect most of the faces I meet to be the faces of strangers. (How do you do?) If meetings are quick and impersonal, they have been efficiently managed. I rush past the sounds of voices attending only to the words addressed to me. Voices seem planed to an even surface of sound, soundless. A business associate speaks in a deep baritone, but I pass through the timbre to attend to his words. The crazy man who sells me a newspaper every night mumbles something crazy, but I have time only to pretend that I have heard him say hello. Accented versions of English make little impression on me. In the rush-hour crowd a Japanese tourist asks me a question, and I inch past his accent to concentrate on what he is saying. The Eastern European immigrant in a neighborhood delicatessen speaks to me through a marinade of sounds, but I respond to his words. I note for only a second the Texas accent of the telephone operator or the Mississippi accent of the man who lives in the apartment below me.

My city seems silent until some ghetto black teenagers board the bus I am on. Because I do not take their presence for granted, I listen to the sounds of their voices. Of all the accented versions of English I hear in a day, I hear theirs most intently. They are *the* sounds of the outsider. They annoy me for being loud – so self-sufficient and unconcerned by my presence. Yet for the same reason they seem to me glamorous. (A romantic gesture against public acceptance.) Listening to their shouted laughter, I realize my own quiet. Their voices enclose my isolation. I feel envious, envious of their brazen intimacy.

I warn myself away from such envy, however. I remember the black political activists who have argued in favor of using black English in schools. (Their argument varies only slightly from that made by foreign-language bilingualists.) I have heard 'radical' linguists make the point that black English is a complex and intricate version of English. And I do not doubt it. But neither do I think that black English should be a language of public instruction. What makes black English inappropriate in classrooms is not something *in* the language. It is rather what lower-class speakers make of it. Just as Spanish would have been a dangerous language for me to have used at the start of my education, so black English would be a dangerous language to use in the schooling of teenagers for whom it reenforces feelings of public separateness.

This seems to me an obvious point. But one that needs to be made. In recent years there have been attempts to make the language of the alien public language. 'Bilingual education, two ways to understand . . . ,' television and radio commercials glibly announce. Proponents of bilingual education are careful to say that they want students to acquire good schooling. Their argument goes something like this: Children permitted to use their family language in school will not be so alienated and will be better able to match the progress of English-speaking children in the crucial first months of instruction. (Increasingly confident of their abilities, such children will be more inclined to apply themselves to their studies in the future.) But then the bilingualists claim another, very different goal. They say that children who use their family language in school will retain a sense of their individuality – their ethnic heritage and cultural ties. Supporters of bilingual education thus want it both ways. They propose bilingual schooling as a way of helping students acquire the skills of the classroom crucial for public success. But they likewise insist that bilingual instruction will give students a sense of their identity apart from the public.

Behind this screen there gleams an astonishing promise: One can become a public person while still remaining a private person. At the very same time one can be both! There need be no tension between the self in the crowd and the self apart from the crowd! Who would not want to believe such an idea? Who can be surprised that the scheme has won the support of many middle-class Americans? If the barrio or ghetto child can retain his separateness even while being publicly educated, then it is almost possible to believe that there is no private cost to be paid for public success. Such is the consolation offered by any of the current bilingual schemes. Consider, for example, the bilingual voters' ballot. In some American cities one can cast a ballot printed in several languages. Such a document implies that a person can exercise that most public of rights – the right to vote – while still keeping apart, unassimilated from public life.

It is not enough to say that these schemes are foolish and certainly doomed. Middle-class supporters of public bilingualism toy with the confusion of those Americans who cannot speak standard English as well as they can. Bilingual enthusiasts, moreover, sin against intimacy. An Hispanic-American writer tells me, 'I will never give up my family language; I would as soon give up my soul.' Thus he holds to his chest a skein of words, as though it were the source of his family ties. He credits to language what he should credit to family members. A convenient mistake. For as long as he holds on to words, he can ignore how much else has changed in his life.

It has happened before. In earlier decades, persons newly successful and ambitious for social mobility similarly seized upon certain 'family words.' Working-class men attempting political power took to calling one another 'brother.' By so doing they escaped oppressive public isolation and were able to unite with many others like themselves. But they paid a price for this union. It was a public union they forged. The word they coined to address one another could never be the sound (*brother*) exchanged by two in intimate greeting. In the union hall the word 'brother' became a vague metaphor; with repetition a weak echo of the intimate sound. Context forced the change. Context could not be overruled. Context will always guard the realm of the intimate from public misuse.

Today nonwhite Americans call 'brother' to strangers. And white feminists refer to their mass union of 'sisters.' And white middle-class teenagers continue to prove the importance of context as they try to ignore it. They seize upon the idioms of the black ghetto. But their attempt to appropriate such expressions invariably changes the words. As it becomes a public expression, the ghetto idiom loses its sound – its message of public separateness and strident intimacy. It becomes with public repetition a series of words, increasingly lifeless.

The mystery remains: intimate utterance. The communication of intimacy passes through the word to enliven its sound. But it cannot be held by the word. Cannot be clutched or ever quoted. It is too fluid. It depends not on word but on person.

My grandmother!

She stood among my other relations mocking me when I no longer spoke Spanish. '*Pocho*,' she said. But then it made no difference. (She'd laugh.) Our relationship continued. Language was never its source. She was a woman in her eighties during the first decade of my life. A mysterious woman to me, my only living grandparent. A woman of Mexico. The woman in long black dresses that reached down to her shoes. My one relative who spoke no word of English. She had no interest in *gringo* society. She remained completely aloof from the public. Protected by her daughters. Protected even by me when we went to Safeway together and I acted as her translator. Eccentric woman. Soft. Hard.

When my family visited my aunt's house in San Francisco, my grandmother searched for me among my many cousins. She'd chase them away. Pinching her granddaughters, she'd warn them all away from me. Then she'd take me to her room, where she had prepared for my coming. There would be a chair next to the bed. A dusty jellied candy nearby. And a copy of *Life en Español* for me to examine. 'There,' she'd say. I'd sit there content. A boy of eight. *Pocho.* Her favorite. I'd sift through the pictures of earthquake-destroyed Latin American cities and blond-wigged Mexican movie stars. And all the while I'd listen to the sound of my grandmother's voice. She'd pace round the room, searching through closets and drawers, telling me stories of her life. Her past. They were stories so familiar to me that I couldn't remember the first time I'd heard them. I'd look up sometimes to listen. Other times she'd look over at me. But she never seemed to expect a response. Sometimes I'd smile or nod. (I understood exactly what she was saying.) But it never seemed to matter to her one way or another. It was enough I was there. The words she spoke were almost irrelevant to that fact – the sounds she made. Content.

The mystery remained: intimate utterance.

I learn little about language and intimacy listening to those social activists who propose using one's family language in public life. Listening to songs on the radio, or hearing a great voice at the opera, or overhearing the woman downstairs singing to herself at an open window, I learn much more. Singers celebrate the human voice. Their lyrics are words. But animated by voice those words are subsumed into sounds. I listen with excitement as the words yield their enormous power to sound – though the words are never totally obliterated. In most songs the drama or tension results from the fact that the singer moves between word (sense) and note (song). At one moment the song simply 'says' something. At another moment the voice stretches out the words – the heart cannot contain! – and the voice moves toward pure sound. Words take flight.

Singing out words, the singer suggests an experience of sound most intensely mine at intimate moments. Literally, most songs are about love. (Lost love; celebrations of loving; pleas.) By simply being occasions when sound escapes word, however, songs put me in mind of the most intimate moments of my life.

Finally, among all types of song, it is the song created by lyric poets that I find most compelling. There is no other public occasion of sound so important for me. Written poems exist on a page, at first glance, as a mere collection of words. And yet, despite this, without musical accompaniment, the poet leads me to hear the sounds of the words that I read. As song, the poem passes between sound and sense, never belonging for long to one realm or the other. As public artifact, the poem can never duplicate intimate sound. But by imitating such sound, the poem helps me recall the intimate times of my life. I read in my room – alone – and grow conscious of being alone, sounding my voice, in search of another. The poem serves then as a memory device. It forces remembrance. And refreshes. It reminds me of the possibility of escaping public words, the possibility that awaits me in meeting the intimate.

The poems I read are not nonsense poems. But I read them for reasons which, I imagine, are similar to those that make children play with meaningless rhyme. I have watched them before: I have noticed the way children create private languages to keep away the adult; I have heard their chanting riddles that go nowhere in logic but harken back to some kingdom of sound; I have watched them listen to intricate nonsense rhymes, and I have noted their wonder. I was never such a child. Until I was six years old, I remained in a magical realm of sound. I didn't need to remember that realm because it was present to me. But then the screen door shut behind me as I left home for school. At last I began my movement toward words. On the other side of initial sadness would come the realization that intimacy cannot be held. With time would come the knowledge that intimacy must finally pass.

I would dishonor those I have loved and those I love now to claim anything else. I would dishonor our closeness by holding on to a particular language and calling it my family language. Intimacy is not trapped within words. It passes through words. It passes. The truth is that intimates leave the room. Doors close. Faces move away from the window. Time passes. Voices recede into the dark. Death finally quiets the voice. And there is no way to deny it. No way to stand in the crowd, uttering one's family language.

The last time I saw my grandmother I was nine years old. I can tell you some of the things she said to me as I stood by her bed. I cannot, however, quote the message of intimacy she conveyed with her voice. She laughed, holding my hand. Her voice illumined disjointed memories as it passed them again. She remembered her husband, his green eyes, the magic name of Narciso. His early death. She remembered the farm in Mexico. The eucalyptus nearby. (Its scent, she remembered, like incense.) She remembered the family cow, the bell round its neck heard miles away. A dog. She remembered working as a seamstress. How she'd leave her daughters and son for long hours to go into Guadalajara to work. And how my mother would come running toward her in the sun – her bright yellow dress – to see her return. '*Mmmaaammmmmáááá*,' the old lady mimicked her daughter (my mother) to her son. She laughed. There was the snap of a cough. An aunt came into the room and told me it was time I should leave. 'You can see her tomorrow,' she promised. And so I kissed my grandmother's cracked face. And the last thing I saw was her thin, oddly youthful thigh, as my aunt rearranged the sheet on the bed.

At the funeral parlor a few days after, I knelt with my relatives during the rosary. Among their voices but silent, I traced, then lost, the sounds of individual aunts in the surge of the common prayer. And I heard at that moment what I have since heard often again – the sounds the women in my family make when they are praying in sadness. When I went up to look at my grandmother, I saw her through the haze of a veil draped over the open lid of the casket. Her face appeared calm – but distant and unyielding to love. It was not the face I remembered seeing most often. It was the face she made in public when the clerk at Safeway asked her some question and I would have to respond. It was her public face the mortician had designed with his dubious art.

TWO

The Achievement of Desire

I stand in the ghetto classroom – 'the guest speaker' – attempting to lecture on the mystery of the sounds of our words to rows of diffident students. 'Don't you hear it? Listen! The music of our words. "*Sumer is i-cumen in. . . .*" And songs on the car radio. We need Aretha Franklin's voice to fill plain words with music – her life.' In the face of their empty stares, I try to create an enthusiasm. But the girls in the back row turn to watch some boy passing outside. There are flutters of smiles, waves. And someone's mouth elongates heavy, silent words through the barrier of glass. Silent words – the lips straining to shape each voiceless syllable: '*Meet meee late errr.*' By the door, the instructor smiles at me, apparently hoping that I will be able to spark some enthusiasm in the class. But only one student seems to be listening. A girl, maybe fourteen. In this gray room her eyes shine with ambition. She keeps nodding and nodding at all that I say; she even takes notes. And each time I ask a question, she jerks up and down in her desk like a marionette, while her hand waves over the bowed heads of her classmates. It is myself (as a boy) I see as she faces me now (a man in my thirties).

The boy who first entered a classroom barely able to speak English, twenty years later concluded his studies in the stately quiet of the reading room in the British Museum. Thus with one sentence I can summarize my academic career. It will be harder to summarize what sort of life connects the boy to the man.

   With every award, each graduation from one level of education to the next, people I'd meet would congratulate me. Their refrain always the same: 'Your parents must be very proud.' Sometimes then they'd ask me how I managed it – my 'success.'

(How?) After a while, I had several quick answers to give in reply. I'd admit, for one thing, that I went to an excellent grammar school. (My earliest teachers, the nuns, made my success their ambition.) And my brother and both my sisters were very good students. (They often brought home the shiny school trophies I came to want.) And my mother and father always encouraged me. (At every graduation they were behind the stunning flash of the camera when I turned to look at the crowd.)

As important as these factors were, however, they account inadequately for my academic advance. Nor do they suggest what an odd success I managed. For although I was a very good student, I was also a very bad student. I was a 'scholarship boy,' a certain kind of scholarship boy. Always successful, I was always unconfident. Exhilarated by my progress. Sad. I became the prized student – anxious and eager to learn. Too eager, too anxious – an imitative and unoriginal pupil. My brother and two sisters enjoyed the advantages I did, and they grew to be as successful as I, but none of them ever seemed so anxious about their schooling. A second-grade student, I was the one who came home and corrected the 'simple' grammatical mistakes of our parents. ('Two negatives make a positive.') Proudly I announced – to my family's startled silence – that a teacher had said I was losing all trace of a Spanish accent. I was oddly annoyed when I was unable to get parental help with a homework assignment. The night my father tried to help me with an arithmetic exercise, he kept reading the instructions, each time more deliberately, until I pried the textbook out of his hands, saying, 'I'll try to figure it out some more by myself.'

When I reached the third grade, I outgrew such behavior. I became more tactful, careful to keep separate the two very different worlds of my day. But then, with ever-increasing intensity, I devoted myself to my studies. I became bookish, puzzling to all my family. Ambition set me apart. When my brother saw me struggling home with stacks of library books, he would laugh, shouting: 'Hey, Four Eyes!' My father opened a closet one day and was startled to find me inside, reading a novel. My mother would find me reading when I was supposed to be asleep or helping around the house or playing outside. In a voice angry or worried or just curious, she'd ask: 'What do you see in your books?' It became the family's joke. When I was called and wouldn't reply, someone would say I must be hiding under my bed with a book.

(How did I manage my success?)

What I am about to say to you has taken me more than twenty years to admit: *A primary reason for my success in the classroom was that I couldn't forget that schooling was changing me and separating me from the life I enjoyed before becoming a student.* That simple realization! For years I never spoke to anyone about it. Never mentioned a thing to my family or my teachers or classmates. From a very early age, I understood enough, just enough about my classroom experiences to keep what I knew repressed, hidden beneath layers of embarrassment. Not until my last months as a graduate student, nearly thirty years old, was it possible for me to think much about the reasons for my academic success. Only then. At the end of my schooling, I needed to determine how far I had moved from my past. The adult finally confronted, and now must publicly say, what the child shuddered from knowing and could never admit to himself or to those many faces that smiled at his every success. ('Your parents must be very proud. . . .')

I

At the end, in the British Museum (too distracted to finish my dissertation) for weeks I read, speed-read, books by modern educational theorists, only to find infrequent and slight mention of students like me. (Much more is written about the more typical case, the lower-class student who barely is helped by his schooling.) Then one day, leafing through Richard Hoggart's *The Uses of Literacy*, I found, in his description of the scholarship boy, myself. For the first time I realized that there were other students like me, and so I was able to frame the meaning of my academic success, its consequent price – the loss.

Hoggart's description is distinguished, at least initially, by deep understanding. What he grasps very well is that the scholarship boy must move between environments, his home and the classroom, which are at cultural extremes, opposed. With his family, the boy has the intense pleasure of intimacy, the family's consolation in feeling public alienation. Lavish emotions texture home life. *Then*, at school, the instruction bids him to trust lonely reason primarily. Immediate needs set the pace of his parents' lives. From his mother and father the boy learns to trust spontaneity and nonrational ways of knowing. *Then*, at school, there is mental calm. Teachers emphasize the value of a reflectiveness that opens a space between thinking and immediate action.

Years of schooling must pass before the boy will be able to sketch the cultural differences in his day as abstractly as this. But he senses those differences early. Perhaps as early as the night he brings home an assignment from school and finds the house too noisy for study.

He has to be more and more alone, if he is going to 'get on'. He will have, probably unconsciously, to oppose the ethos of the hearth, the intense gregariousness of the working-class family group. Since everything centres upon the living-room, there is unlikely to be a room of his own; the bedrooms are cold and inhospitable, and to warm them or the front room, if there is one, would not only be expensive, but would require an imaginative leap – out of the tradition – which most families are not capable of making. There is a corner of the living-room table. On the other side Mother is ironing, the wireless is on, someone is singing a snatch of song or Father says intermittently whatever comes into his head. The boy has to cut himself off mentally, so as to do his homework, as well as he can.*

The next day, the lesson is as apparent at school. There are even rows of desks. Discussion is ordered. The boy must rehearse his thoughts and raise his hand before speaking out in a loud voice to an audience of classmates. And there is time enough, and silence, to think about ideas (big ideas) never considered at home by his parents.

Not for the working-class child alone is adjustment to the classroom difficult. Good schooling requires that any student alter early childhood habits. But the working-class child is usually least prepared for the change. And, unlike many middle-class children, he goes home and sees in his parents a way of life not only different but starkly opposed to that of the classroom. (He enters the house and hears his parents talking in ways his teachers discourage.)

Without extraordinary determination and the great assistance of others – at home and at school – there is little chance for success. Typically most working-class children are barely

---

* All quotations in this chapter are from Richard Hoggart, *The Uses of Literacy* (London: Chatto and Windus, 1957), chapter 10.

changed by the classroom. The exception succeeds. The relative few become scholarship students. Of these, Richard Hoggart estimates, most manage a fairly graceful transition. Somehow they learn to live in the two very different worlds of their day. There are some others, however, those Hoggart pejoratively terms 'scholarship boys,' for whom success comes with special anxiety. Scholarship boy: good student, troubled son. The child is 'moderately endowed,' intellectually mediocre, Hoggart supposes – though it may be more pertinent to note the special qualities of temperament in the child. High-strung child. Brooding. Sensitive. Haunted by the knowledge that one *chooses* to become a student. (Education is not an inevitable or natural step in growing up.) Here is a child who cannot forget that his academic success distances him from a life he loved, even from his own memory of himself.

Initially, he wavers, balances allegiance. ('The boy is himself [until he reaches, say, the upper forms] very much of *both* the worlds of home and school. He is enormously obedient to the dictates of the world of school, but emotionally still strongly wants to continue as part of the family circle.') Gradually, necessarily, the balance is lost. The boy needs to spend more and more time studying, each night enclosing himself in the silence permitted and required by intense concentration. He takes his first step toward academic success, away from his family.

From the very first days, through the years following, it will be with his parents – the figures of lost authority, the persons toward whom he feels deepest love – that the change will be most powerfully measured. A separation will unravel between them. Advancing in his studies, the boy notices that his mother and father have not changed as much as he. Rather, when he sees them, they often remind him of the person he once was and the life he earlier shared with them. He realizes what some Romantics also know when they praise the working class for the capacity for human closeness, qualities of passion and spontaneity, that the rest of us experience in like measure only in the earliest part of our youth. For the Romantic, this doesn't make working-class life childish. Working-class life challenges precisely because it is an *adult* way of life.

The scholarship boy reaches a different conclusion. He cannot afford to admire his parents. (How could he and still pursue such a contrary life?) He permits himself embarrassment at their lack of education. And to evade nostalgia for the life he has lost, he concentrates on the benefits education will bestow upon him. He becomes especially ambitious. Without the support of old certainties and consolations, almost mechanically, he assumes the procedures and doctrines of the classroom. The kind of allegiance the young student might have given his mother and father only days earlier, he transfers to the teacher, the new figure of authority. '[The scholarship boy] tends to make a father-figure of his form-master,' Hoggart observes.

But Hoggart's calm prose only makes me recall the urgency with which I came to idolize my grammar school teachers. I began by imitating their accents, using their diction, trusting their every direction. The very first facts they dispensed, I grasped with awe. Any book they told me to read, I read – then waited for them to tell me which books I enjoyed. Their every casual opinion I came to adopt and to trumpet when I returned home. I stayed after school 'to help' – to get my teacher's undivided attention. It was the nun's encouragement that mattered most to me. (She understood exactly what – my parents never seemed to appraise so well – all my achievements entailed.)

After a while, I grew more calm at home. I developed tact. A fourth-grade student, I was no longer the show-off in front of my parents. I became a conventionally dutiful son, politely affectionate, cheerful enough, even – for reasons beyond choosing – my father's favorite. And much about my family life was easy then, comfortable, happy in the rhythm of our living together: hearing my father getting ready for work; eating the breakfast my mother had made me; looking up from a novel to hear my brother or one of my sisters playing with friends in the backyard; in winter, coming upon the house all lighted up after dark.

But withheld from my mother and father was any mention of what most mattered to me: the extraordinary experience of first-learning. Late afternoon: In the midst of preparing dinner, my mother would come up behind me while I was trying to read. Her head just over mine, her breath warmly scented with food. 'What are you reading?' Or, 'Tell me all about your new courses.' I would barely respond, 'Just the usual things, nothing special.' (A half smile, then silence. Her head moving back in the silence. Silence! Instead of the flood of intimate sounds that had once flowed smoothly between us, there was this silence.) After dinner, I would rush to a bedroom with papers and books. As often as possible, I resisted parental pleas to 'save lights' by coming to the kitchen to work. I kept so much, so often, to myself. Sad. Enthusiastic. Troubled by the excitement of coming upon new ideas. Eager. Fascinated by the promising texture of a brand-new book. I hoarded the pleasures of learning. Alone for hours. Enthralled. Nervous. I rarely looked away from my books – or back on my memories. Nights when relatives visited and the front rooms were warmed by Spanish sounds, I slipped quietly out of the house.

It mattered that education was changing me. It never ceased to matter. My brother and sisters would giggle at our mother's mispronounced words. They'd correct her gently. My mother laughed girlishly one night, trying not to pronounce *sheep* as *ship*. From a distance I listened sullenly. From that distance, pretending not to notice on another occasion, I saw my father looking at the title pages of my library books. That was the scene on my mind when I walked home with a fourth-grade companion and heard him say that his parents read to him every night. (A strange-sounding book – *Winnie the Pooh*.) Immediately, I wanted to know, 'What is it like?' My companion, however, thought I wanted to know about the plot of the book. Another day, my mother surprised me by asking for a 'nice' book to read. 'Something not too hard you think I might like.' Carefully I chose one, Willa Cather's *My Ántonia*. But when, several weeks later, I happened to see it next to her bed unread except for the first few pages, I was furious and suddenly wanted to cry. I grabbed up the book and took it back to my room and placed it in its place, alphabetically on my shelf.

'Your parents must be very proud of you.' People began to say that to me about the time I was in sixth grade. To answer affirmatively, I'd smile. Shyly I'd smile, never betraying my sense of the irony: I was not proud of my mother and father. I was embarrassed by their lack of education. It was not that I ever thought they were stupid, though stupidly I took for granted their enormous native intelligence. Simply, what mattered to me was that they were not like my teachers.

But, 'Why didn't you tell us about the award?' my mother demanded, her frown weakened by pride. At the grammar school ceremony several weeks after, her eyes were brighter than the trophy I'd won. Pushing back the hair from my forehead, she whispered that I had 'shown' the *gringos*. A few minutes later, I heard my father speak to my teacher and felt ashamed of his labored, accented words. Then guilty for the shame. I felt such contrary feelings. (There is no simple roadmap through the heart of the scholarship boy.) My teacher was so soft-spoken and her words were edged sharp and clean. I admired her until it seemed to me that she spoke too carefully. Sensing that she was condescending to them, I became nervous. Resentful. Protective. I tried to move my parents away. 'You both must be very proud of Richard,' the nun said. They responded quickly. (They were proud.) 'We are proud of all our children.' Then this afterthought: 'They sure didn't get their brains from us.' They all laughed. I smiled.

Tightening the irony into a knot was the knowledge that my parents were always behind me. They made success possible. They evened the path. They sent their children to parochial schools because the nuns 'teach better.' They paid a tuition they couldn't afford. They spoke English to us.

For their children my parents wanted chances they never had – an easier way. It saddened my mother to learn that some relatives forced their children to start working right after high school. To *her* children she would say, 'Get all the education you can.' In schooling she recognized the key to job advancement. And with the remark she remembered her past.

As a girl new to America my mother had been awarded a high school diploma by teachers too careless or busy to notice that she hardly spoke English. On her own, she determined to learn how to type. That skill got her jobs typing envelopes in letter shops, and it encouraged in her an optimism about the possibility of advancement. (Each morning when her sisters put on uniforms, she chose a bright-colored dress.) The years of young womanhood passed, and her typing speed increased. She also became an excellent speller of words she mispronounced. 'And I've never been to college,' she'd say, smiling, when her children asked her to spell words they were too lazy to look up in a dictionary.

Typing, however, was dead-end work. Finally frustrating. When her youngest child started high school, my mother got a full-time office job once again. (Her paycheck combined with my father's to make us – in fact – what we had already become in our imagination of ourselves – middle class.) She worked then for the (California) state government in numbered civil service positions secured by examinations. The old ambition of her youth was rekindled. During the lunch hour, she consulted bulletin boards for announcements of openings. One day she saw mention of something called an 'anti-poverty agency.' A typing job. A glamorous job, part of the governor's staff. 'A knowledge of Spanish required.' Without hesitation she applied and became nervous only when the job was suddenly hers.

'Everyone comes to work all dressed up,' she reported at night. And didn't need to say more than that her co-workers wouldn't let her answer the phones. She was only a typist, after all, albeit a very fast typist. And an excellent speller. One morning there was a letter to be sent to a Washington cabinet officer. On the dictating tape, a voice referred to urban guerrillas. My mother typed (the wrong word, correctly): 'gorillas.' The mistake horrified the anti-poverty bureaucrats who shortly after arranged to have her returned to her previous position. She would go no further. So she willed her ambition to her children. 'Get all the education you can; with an education you can do anything.' (With a good education *she* could have done anything.)

When I was in high school, I admitted to my mother that I planned to become a teacher someday. That seemed to please her. But I never tried to explain that it was not the occupation of teaching I yearned for as much as it was something more elusive: I wanted to *be* like my teachers, to possess their knowledge, to assume their authority, their confidence, even to assume a teacher's persona.

In contrast to my mother, my father never verbally encouraged his children's academic success. Nor did he often praise us. My mother had to remind him to 'say something' to one of his children who scored some academic success. But whereas my mother saw in education the opportunity for job advancement, my father recognized that education provided an even more startling possibility: It could enable a person to escape from a life of mere labor.

In Mexico, orphaned when he was eight, my father left school to work as an 'apprentice' for an uncle. Twelve years later, he left Mexico in frustration and arrived in America. He had great expectations then of becoming an engineer. ('Work for my hands and my head.') He knew a Catholic priest who promised to get him money enough to study full time for a high school diploma. But the promises came to nothing. Instead there was a dark succession of warehouse, cannery, and factory jobs. After work he went to night school along with my mother. A year, two passed. Nothing much changed, except that fatigue worked its way into the bone; then everything changed. He didn't talk anymore of becoming an engineer. He stayed outside on the steps of the school while my mother went inside to learn typing and shorthand.

By the time I was born, my father worked at 'clean' jobs. For a time he was a janitor at a fancy department store. ('Easy work; the machines do it all.') Later he became a dental technician. ('Simple.') But by then he was pessimistic about the ultimate meaning of work and the possibility of ever escaping its claims. In some of my earliest memories of him, my father already seems aged by fatigue. (He has never really grown old like my mother.) From boyhood to manhood, I have remembered him in a single image: seated, asleep on the sofa, his head thrown back in a hideous corpselike grin, the evening newspaper spread out before him. 'But look at all you've accomplished,' his best friend said to him once. My father said nothing. Only smiled.

It was my father who laughed when I claimed to be tired by reading and writing. It was he who teased me for having soft hands. (He seemed to sense that some great achievement of leisure was implied by my papers and books.) It was my father who became angry while watching on television some woman at the Miss America contest tell the announcer that she was going to college. ('Majoring in fine arts.') 'College!' he snarled. He despised the trivialization of higher education, the inflated grades and cheapened diplomas, the half education that so often passed as mass education in my generation.

It was my father again who wondered why I didn't display my awards on the wall of my bedroom. He said he liked to go to doctors' offices and see their certificates and degrees on the wall. ('Nice.') My citations from school got left in closets at home. The gleaming figure astride one of my trophies was broken, wingless, after hitting the ground. My medals were placed in a jar of loose change. And when I lost my high school diploma, my father found it as it was about to be thrown out with the trash. Without telling me, he put it away with his own things for safekeeping.

These memories slammed together at the instant of hearing that refrain familiar to all scholarship students: 'Your parents must be very proud. . . .' Yes, my parents were proud. I knew it. But my parents regarded my progress with more than mere pride. They endured my early precocious behavior – but with what private anger and humiliation? As their children got older and would come home to challenge ideas both of them held, they argued before submitting to the force of logic or superior factual evidence with the disclaimer, 'It's what we were taught in our time to believe.' These discussions ended abruptly, though my mother remembered them on other occasions when she complained that our 'big ideas' were going to our heads. More acute was her complaint that the family wasn't close any-more, like some others she knew. Why weren't we close, 'more in the Mexican style'? Everyone is so private, she added. And she mimicked the yes and no answers she got in reply to her questions. Why didn't we talk more? (My father never asked.) I never said.

I was the first in my family who asked to leave home when it came time to go to college. I had been admitted to Stanford, one hundred miles away. My departure would only make phys-ically apparent the separation that had occurred long before. But it was going too far. In the months preceding my leaving, I heard the question my mother never asked except indirectly. In the hot kitchen, tired at the end of her workday, she de-manded to know, 'Why aren't the colleges here in Sacramento good enough for you? They are for your brother and sister.' In the middle of a car ride, not turning to face me, she wondered, 'Why do you need to go so far away?' Late at night, ironing, she said with disgust, 'Why do you have to put us through this big expense? You know your scholarship will never cover it all.' But when September came there was a rush to get everything ready. In a bedroom that last night I packed the big brown valise, and my mother sat nearby sewing initials onto the clothes I would take. And she said no more about my leaving.

Months later, two weeks of Christmas vacation: The first hours home were the hardest. ('What's new?') My parents and I sat in the kitchen for a conversation. (But, lacking the same words to develop our sentences and to shape our interests, what was there to say? What could I tell them of the term paper I had just finished on the 'universality of Shakespeare's appeal'?) I mentioned only small, obvious things: my dormitory life; weekend trips I had taken; random events. They responded with news of their own. (One was almost grateful for a family crisis about which there was much to discuss.) We tried to make our conversation seem like more than an interview.

2

From an early age I knew that my mother and father could read and write both Spanish and English. I had observed my father making his way through what, I now suppose, must have been income tax forms. On other occasions I waited apprehensively while my mother read onion-paper letters airmailed from Mexico with news of a relative's illness or death. For both my parents, however, reading was something done out of necessity and as quickly as possible. Never did I see either of them read an entire book. Nor did I see them read for pleasure. Their reading consisted of work manuals, prayer books, newspapers, recipes.

Richard Hoggart imagines how, at home,

... [The scholarship boy] sees strewn around, and reads regularly himself, magazines which are never mentioned at school, which seem not to belong to the world to which the school introduces him; at school he hears about and reads books never mentioned at home. When he brings those books into the house they do not take their place with other books which the family are reading, for often there are none or almost none; his books look, rather, like strange tools.

In our house each school year would begin with my mother's careful instruction: 'Don't write in your books so we can sell them at the end of the year.' The remark was echoed in public by my teachers, but only in part: 'Boys and girls, don't write in your books. You must learn to treat them with great care and respect.'

OPEN THE DOORS OF YOUR MIND WITH BOOKS, read the red and white poster over the nun's desk in early September. It soon was apparent to me that reading was the classroom's central activity. Each course had its own book. And the information gathered from a book was unquestioned. READ TO LEARN, the sign on the wall advised in December. I privately wondered: What was the connection between reading and learning? Did one learn something only by reading it? Was an idea only an idea if it could be written down? In June, CONSIDER BOOKS YOUR BEST FRIENDS. Friends? Reading was, at best, only a chore. I needed to look up whole paragraphs of words in a dictionary. Lines of type were dizzying, the eye having to move slowly across the page, then down, and across ... The sentences of the first books I read were coolly impersonal. Toned hard. What most bothered me, however, was the isolation reading required. To console myself for the loneliness I'd feel when I read, I tried reading in a very soft voice. Until: 'Who is doing all that talking to his neighbor?' Shortly after, remedial reading classes were arranged for me with a very old nun.

At the end of each school day, for nearly six months, I would meet with her in the tiny room that served as the school's library but was actually only a storeroom for used textbooks and a vast collection of *National Geographics*. Everything about our sessions pleased me: the smallness of the room; the noise of the janitor's broom hitting the edge of the long hallway outside the door; the green of the sun, lighting the wall; and the old woman's face blurred white with a beard. Most of the time we took turns. I began with my elementary text. Sentences of astonishing simplicity seemed to me lifeless and drab: 'The boys ran from the rain . . . She wanted to sing . . . The kite rose in the blue.' Then the old nun would read from her favorite books, usually biographies of early American presidents. Playfully she ran through complex sentences, calling the words alive with her voice, making it seem that the author somehow was speaking directly to me. I smiled just to listen to her. I sat there and sensed for the very first time some possibility of fellowship between a reader and a writer, a communication, never *intimate* like that I heard spoken words at home convey, but one nonetheless *personal*.

One day the nun concluded a session by asking me why I was so reluctant to read by myself. I tried to explain; said something about the way written words made me feel all alone – almost, I wanted to add but didn't, as when I spoke to myself in a room just emptied of furniture. She studied my face as I spoke; she seemed to be watching more than listening. In an uneventful voice she replied that I had nothing to fear. Didn't I realize that reading would open up whole new worlds? A book could open doors for me. It could introduce me to people and show me places I never imagined existed. She gestured toward the bookshelves. (Bare-breasted African women danced, and the shiny hubcaps of automobiles on the back covers of the *Geographic* gleamed in my mind.) I listened with respect. But her words were not very influential. I was thinking then of another consequence of literacy, one I was too shy to admit but nonetheless trusted. Books were going to make me 'educated.' *That* confidence enabled me, several months later, to overcome my fear of the silence.

In fourth grade I embarked upon a grandiose reading program. 'Give me the names of important books,' I would say to startled teachers. They soon found out that I had in mind 'adult books.' I ignored their suggestion of anything I suspected was written for children. (Not until I was in college, as a result, did I read *Huckleberry Finn* or *Alice's Adventures in Wonderland*.) Instead, I read *The Scarlet Letter* and Franklin's *Autobiography*. And whatever I read I read for extra credit. Each time I finished a book, I reported the achievement to a teacher and basked in the praise my effort earned. Despite my best efforts, however, there seemed to be more and more books I needed to read. At the library I would literally tremble as I came upon whole shelves of books I hadn't read. So I read and I read and I read: *Great Expectations*; all the short stories of Kipling; *The Babe Ruth Story*; the entire first volume of the *Encyclopaedia Britannica* (A-ANSTEY); the *Iliad*; *Moby Dick*; *Gone with the Wind*; *The Good Earth*; *Ramona*; *Forever Amber*; *The Lives of the Saints*; *Crime and Punishment*; *The Pearl*. . . . Librarians who initially frowned when I checked out the maximum ten books at a time started saving books they thought I might like. Teachers would say to the rest of the class, 'I only wish the rest of you took reading as seriously as Richard obviously does.'

But at home I would hear my mother wondering, 'What do you see in your books?' (Was reading a hobby like her knitting? Was so much reading even healthy for a boy? Was it the sign of 'brains'? Or was it just a convenient excuse for not helping around the house on Saturday mornings?) Always, 'What do you see . . . ?'

What *did* I see in my books? I had the idea that they were crucial for my academic success, though I couldn't have said exactly how or why. In the sixth grade I simply concluded that what gave a book its value was some major idea or theme it contained. If that core essence could be mined and memorized, I would become learned like my teachers. I decided to record in a notebook the themes of the books that I read. After reading *Robinson Crusoe*, I wrote that its theme was 'the value of learning to live by oneself.' When I completed *Wuthering Heights*, I noted the danger of 'letting emotions get out of control.' Rereading these brief moralistic appraisals usually left me disheartened. I couldn't believe that they were really the source of reading's value. But for many more years, they constituted the only means I had of describing to myself the educational value of books.

In spite of my earnestness, I found reading a pleasurable activity. I came to enjoy the lonely good company of books. Early on weekday mornings, I'd read in my bed. I'd feel a mysterious comfort then, reading in the dawn quiet – the blue-gray silence interrupted by the occasional churning of the refrigerator motor a few rooms away or the more distant sounds of a city bus beginning its run. On weekends I'd go to the public library to read, surrounded by old men and women. Or, if the weather was fine, I would take my books to the park and read in the shade of a tree. A warm summer evening was my favorite reading time. Neighbors would leave for vacation and I would water their lawns. I would sit through the twilight on the front porches or in backyards, reading to the cool, whirling sounds of the sprinklers.

I also had favorite writers. But often those writers I enjoyed most I was least able to value. When I read William Saroyan's *The Human Comedy*, I was immediately pleased by the narrator's warmth and the charm of his story. But as quickly I became suspicious. A book so enjoyable to read couldn't be very 'important.' Another summer I determined to read all the novels of Dickens. Reading his fat novels, I loved the feeling I got – after the first hundred pages – of being at home in a fictional world where I knew the names of the characters and cared about what was going to happen to them. And it bothered me that I was forced away at the conclusion, when the fiction closed tight, like a fortune-teller's fist – the futures of all the major characters neatly resolved. I never knew how to take such feelings seriously, however. Nor did I suspect that these experiences could be part of a novel's meaning. Still, there were pleasures to sustain me after I'd finish my books. Carrying a volume back to the library, I would be pleased by its weight. I'd run my fingers along the edge of the pages and marvel at the breadth of my achievement. Around my room, growing stacks of paperback books reenforced my assurance.

I entered high school having read hundreds of books. My habit of reading made me a confident speaker and writer of English. Reading also enabled me to sense something of the shape, the major concerns, of Western thought. (I was able to say something about Dante and Descartes and Engels and James Baldwin in my high school term papers.) In these various ways, books brought me academic success as I hoped that they would. But I was not a good reader. Merely bookish, I lacked a point of view when I read. Rather, I read in order to acquire a point of view. I vacuumed books for epigrams, scraps of information, ideas, themes – anything to fill the hollow within me and make me feel educated. When one of my teachers suggested to his drowsy tenth-grade English class that a person could not have a 'complicated idea' until he had read at least two thousand books, I heard the remark without detecting either its irony or its very complicated truth. I merely determined to compile a list of all the books I had ever read. Harsh with myself, I included only once a title I might have read several times. (How, after all, could one read a book more than once?) And I included only those books over a hundred pages in length. (Could anything shorter be a book?)

There was yet another high school list I compiled. One day I came across a newspaper article about the retirement of an English professor at a nearby state college. The article was accompanied by a list of the 'hundred most important books of Western Civilization.' 'More than anything else in my life,' the professor told the reporter with finality, 'these books have made me all that I am.' That was the kind of remark I couldn't ignore. I clipped out the list and kept it for the several months it took me to read all of the titles. Most books, of course, I barely understood. While reading Plato's *Republic*, for instance, I needed to keep looking at the book jacket comments to remind myself what the text was about. Nevertheless, with the special patience and superstition of a scholarship boy, I looked at every word of the text. And by the time I reached the last word, relieved, I convinced myself that I had read *The Republic*. In a ceremony of great pride, I solemnly crossed Plato off my list.

3

The scholarship boy pleases most when he is young – the working-class child struggling for academic success. To his teachers, he offers great satisfaction; his success is their proudest achievement. Many other persons offer to help him. A business-man learns the boy's story and promises to underwrite part of the cost of his college education. A woman leaves him her entire library of several hundred books when she moves. His progress is featured in a newspaper article. Many people seem happy for him. They marvel. 'How did you manage so fast?' From all sides, there is lavish praise and encouragement.

In his grammar school classroom, however, the boy already makes students around him uneasy. They scorn his desire to succeed. They scorn him for constantly wanting the teacher's attention and praise. 'Kiss Ass,' they call him when his hand swings up in response to every question he hears. Later, when he makes it to college, no one will mock him aloud. But he detects annoyance on the faces of some students and even some teachers who watch him. It puzzles him often. In college, then in graduate school, he behaves much as he always has. If any-thing is different about him it is that he dares to anticipate the successful conclusion of his studies. At last he feels that he belongs in the classroom, and this is exactly the source of the dissatisfaction he causes. To many persons around him, he ap-pears too much the academic. There may be some things about him that recall his beginnings – his shabby clothes; his persistent poverty; or his dark skin (in those cases when it symbolizes his parents' disadvantaged condition) – but they only make clear how far he has moved from his past. He has used education to remake himself.

It bothers his fellow academics to face this. They will not say why exactly. (They sneer.) But their expectations become obvious when they are disappointed. They expect – they want – a student less changed by his schooling. If the scholarship boy, from a past so distant from the classroom, could remain in some basic way unchanged, he would be able to prove that it is possible for anyone to become educated without basically changing from the person one was.

Here is no fabulous hero, no idealized scholar-worker. The scholarship boy does not straddle, cannot reconcile, the two great opposing cultures of his life. His success is unromantic and plain. He sits in the classroom and offers those sitting beside him no calming reassurance about their own lives. He sits in the seminar room – a man with brown skin, the son of working-class Mexican immigrant parents. (Addressing the professor at the head of the table, his voice catches with nervousness.) There is no trace of his parents' accent in his speech. Instead he approximates the accents of teachers and classmates. Coming from *him* those sounds seem suddenly odd. Odd too is the effect produced when *he* uses academic jargon – bubbles at the tip of his tongue: '*Topos* . . . negative capability . . . vegetation imagery in Shakespearean comedy.' He lifts an opinion from Coleridge, takes something else from Frye or Empson or Leavis. He even repeats exactly his professor's earlier comment. All his ideas are clearly borrowed. He seems to have no thought of his own. He chatters while his listeners smile – their look one of disdain.

When he is older and thus when so little of the person he was survives, the scholarship boy makes only too apparent his profound lack of *self*-confidence. This is the conventional assessment that even Richard Hoggart repeats:

[The scholarship boy] tends to over-stress the importance of examinations, of the piling-up of knowledge and of received opinions. He
discovers a technique of apparent learning, of the acquiring of facts
rather than of the handling and use of facts. He learns how to receive a purely literate education, one using only a small part of the
personality and challenging only a limited area of his being. He be-
gins to see life as a ladder, as a permanent examination with some
praise and some further exhortation at each stage. He becomes an
expert imbiber and doler-out; his competence will vary, but will
rarely be accompanied by genuine enthusiasms. He rarely feels the
reality of knowledge, of other men's thoughts and imaginings, on
his own pulses . . . He has something of the blinkered pony about
him. . . .

But this is criticism more accurate than fair. The scholarship
boy is a very bad student. He is the great mimic; a collector of
thoughts, not a thinker; the very last person in class who ever
feels obliged to have an opinion of his own. In large part, however, the reason he is such a bad student is because he realizes
more often and more acutely than most other students – than
Hoggart himself – that education requires radical self-reforma-
tion. As a very young boy, regarding his parents, as he struggles
with an early homework assignment, he knows this too well.
That is why he lacks self-assurance. He does not forget that the
classroom is responsible for remaking him. He relies on his
teacher, depends on all that he hears in the classroom and reads
in his books. He becomes in every obvious way the worst student, a dummy mouthing the opinions of others. But he would
not be so bad – nor would he become so successful, a *scholarship*
boy – if he did not accurately perceive that the best synonym for
primary 'education' is 'imitation.'

Those who would take seriously the boy's success – and his
failure – would be forced to realize how great is the change any

academic undergoes, how far one must move from one's past. It is easiest to ignore such considerations. So little is said about the scholarship boy in pages and pages of educational literature. Nothing is said of the silence that comes to separate the boy from his parents. Instead, one hears proposals for increasing the self-esteem of students and encouraging early intellectual independence. Paragraphs glitter with a constellation of terms like *creativity* and *originality*. (Ignored altogether is the function of imitation in a student's life.) Radical educationists meanwhile complain that ghetto schools 'oppress' students by trying to mold them, stifling native characteristics. The truer critique would be just the reverse: not that schools change ghetto students too much, but that while they might promote the occasional scholarship student, they change most students barely at all.

From the story of the scholarship boy there is no specific pedagogy to glean. There is, however, a much larger lesson. His story makes clear that education is a long, unglamorous, even demeaning process — *a nurturing never natural to the person one was before one entered a classroom*. At once different from most other students, the scholarship boy is also the archetypal 'good student.' He exaggerates the difficulty of being a student, but his exaggeration reveals a general predicament. Others are changed by their schooling as much as he. They too must re-form themselves. They must develop the skill of memory long before they become truly critical thinkers. And when they read Plato for the first several times, it will be with awe more than deep comprehension.

The impact of schooling on the scholarship boy is only more apparent to the boy himself and to others. Finally, although he may be laughable — a blinkered pony — the boy will not let his critics forget their own change. He ends up too much like them. When he speaks, they hear themselves echoed. In his pedantry, they trace their own. His ambitions are theirs. If his failure were singular, they might readily pity him. But he is more troubling than that. They would not scorn him if this were not so.

4

Like me, Hoggart's imagined scholarship boy spends most of his years in the classroom afraid to long for his past. Only at the very end of his schooling does the boy-man become nostalgic. In this sudden change of heart, Richard Hoggart notes:

He longs for the membership he lost, 'he pines for some Nameless Eden where he never was'. The nostalgia is the stronger and the more ambiguous because he is really 'in quest of his own absconded self yet scared to find it'. He both wants to go back and yet thinks he has gone beyond his class, feels himself weighted with knowledge of his own and their situation, which hereafter forbids him the simpler pleasures of his father and mother. . . .

According to Hoggart, the scholarship boy grows nostalgic because he remains the uncertain scholar, bright enough to have moved from his past, yet unable to feel easy, a part of a community of academics.

This analysis, however, only partially suggests what happened to me in my last year as a graduate student. When I traveled to London to write a dissertation on English Renaissance literature, I was finally confident of membership in a 'community of scholars.' But the pleasure that confidence gave me faded rapidly. After only two or three months in the reading room of the British Museum, it became clear that I had joined a lonely community. Around me each day were dour faces eclipsed by large piles of books. There were the regulars, like the old couple who arrived every morning, each holding a loop of the shopping bag which contained all their notes. And there was the historian who chattered madly to herself. ('Oh dear! Oh! Now, what's this? What? Oh, my!') There were also the faces of young men and women worn by long study. And everywhere eyes turned away the moment our glance accidentally met. Some persons I sat beside day after day, yet we passed silently at the end of the day, strangers. Still, we were united by a common respect for the written word and for scholarship. We did form a union, though one in which we remained distant from one another.

More profound and unsettling was the bond I recognized with those writers whose books I consulted. Whenever I opened a text that hadn't been used for years, I realized that my special interests and skills united me to a mere handful of academics. We formed an exclusive – eccentric! – society, separated from others who would never care or be able to share our concerns. (The pages I turned were stiff like layers of dead skin.) I began to wonder: Who, beside my dissertation director and a few faculty members, would ever read what I wrote? And: Was my dissertation much more than an act of social withdrawal? These questions went unanswered in the silence of the Museum reading room. They remained to trouble me after I'd leave the library each afternoon and feel myself shy – unsteady, speaking simple sentences at the grocer's or the butcher's on my way back to my bed-sitter.

Meanwhile my file cards accumulated. A professional, I knew exactly how to search a book for pertinent information. I could quickly assess and summarize the usability of the many books I consulted. But whenever I started to write, I knew too much (and not enough) to be able to write anything but sentences that were overly cautious, timid, strained brittle under the heavy weight of footnotes and qualifications. I seemed unable to dare a passionate statement. I felt drawn by professionalism to the edge of sterility, capable of no more than pedantic, lifeless, unassailable prose.

Then nostalgia began.

After years spent unwilling to admit its attractions, I gestured nostalgically toward the past. I yearned for that time when I had not been so alone. I became impatient with books. I wanted experience more immediate. I feared the library's silence. I silently scorned the gray, timid faces around me. I grew to hate the growing pages of my dissertation on genre and Renaissance literature. (In my mind I heard relatives laughing as they tried to make sense of its title.) I wanted something – I couldn't say exactly what. I told myself that I wanted a more passionate life. And a life less thoughtful. And above all, I wanted to be less alone. One day I heard some Spanish academics whispering back and forth to each other, and their sounds seemed ghostly voices recalling my life. Yearning became preoccupation then. Boyhood memories beckoned, flooded my mind. (Laughing intimate voices. Bounding up the front steps of the porch. A sudden embrace inside the door.)

For weeks after, I turned to books by educational experts. I needed to learn how far I had moved from my past – to determine how fast I would be able to recover something of it once again. But I found little. Only a chapter in a book by Richard Hoggart . . . I left the reading room and the circle of faces.

I came home. After the year in England, I spent three summer months living with my mother and father, relieved by how easy it was to be home. It no longer seemed very important to me that we had little to say. I felt easy sitting and eating and walking with them. I watched them, nevertheless, looking for evidence of those elastic, sturdy strands that bind generations in a web of inheritance. I thought as I watched my mother one night: Of course a friend had been right when she told me that I gestured and laughed just like my mother. Another time I saw for myself: My father's eyes were much like my own, constantly watchful.

But after the early relief, this return, came suspicion, nagging until I realized that I had not neatly sidestepped the impact of schooling. My desire to do so was precisely the measure of how much I remained an academic. *Negatively* (for that is how this idea first occurred to me): My need to think so much and so abstractly about my parents and our relationship was in itself an indication of my long education. My father and mother did not pass their time thinking about the cultural meanings of their experience. It was I who described their daily lives with airy ideas. And yet, *positively*: The ability to consider experience so abstractly allowed me to shape into desire what would otherwise have remained indefinite, meaningless longing in the British Museum. If, because of my schooling, I had grown culturally separated from my parents, my education finally had given me ways of speaking and caring about that fact.

My best teachers in college and graduate school, years before, had tried to prepare me for this conclusion, I think, when they discussed texts of aristocratic pastoral literature. Faithfully, I wrote down all that they said. I memorized it: 'The praise of the unlettered by the highly educated is one of the primary themes of "elitist" literature.' But, 'the importance of the praise given the unsolitary, richly passionate and spontaneous life is that it simultaneously reflects the value of a reflective life.' I heard it all. But there was no way for any of it to mean very much to me. I was a scholarship boy at the time, busily laddering my way up the rungs of education. To pass an examination, I copied down exactly what my teachers told me. It would require many more years of schooling (an inevitable miseducation) in which I came to trust the silence of reading and the habit of abstracting from immediate experience – moving away from a life of closeness and immediacy I remembered with my parents, growing older – before I turned unafraid to desire the past, and thereby achieved what had eluded me for so long – the end of education.

THREE

Credo

The steps of the church defined the eternal square where children played and adults talked after dinner. He remembers the way the church building was at the center of town life. She remembers the way one could hear the bell throughout the day, telling time. And the way the town completely closed down for certain feastdays. He remembers that the church spire was the first thing he'd see walking back into town. Both my parents have tried to describe something of what it was like for them to have grown up Catholic in small Mexican towns. They remember towns where everyone was a Catholic.

With their move to America, my mother and father left behind that Mexican Church to find themselves (she praying in whispered Spanish) in an Irish-American parish. In a way, they found themselves at ease in such a church. My parents had much in common with the Irish-born priests and nuns. Like my parents, the priests remembered what it was like to have been Catholic in villages and cities where everyone else was a Catholic. In their American classrooms, the nuns worked very hard to approximate that other place, that earlier kind of religious experience. For a time they succeeded. For a time I too enjoyed a Catholicism something like that enjoyed a generation before me by my parents.

I grew up a Catholic at home and at school, in private and in public. My mother and father were deeply pious *católicos*; all my relatives were Catholics. At home, there were holy pictures on a wall of nearly every room, and a crucifix hung over my bed. My first twelve years as a student were spent in Catholic schools where I could look up to the front of the room and see a crucifix hanging over the clock.

When I was a boy, anyone not a Catholic was defined by that fact and the term *non-Catholic*. The expression suggests the parochialism of the Catholicism in which I was raised. In those years I could have told you the names of persons in public life who were Catholics. I knew that Ed Sullivan was a Catholic. And Mrs. Bob Hope. And Senator John F. Kennedy. As the neighborhood newspaper boy, I knew all the names on my route. As a Catholic, I noted which open doors, which front room windows disclosed a crucifix. At quarter to eight Sunday mornings, I saw the O'Briens and the Van Hoyts walking down the empty sidewalk past our house and I knew. Catholics were mysteriously lucky, 'chosen' by God to be nurtured a special way. Non-Catholics had souls too, of course, and somehow could get to heaven. But on Sundays they got all dressed up only to go to a church where there was no incense, no sacred body and blood, and no confessional box. Or else they slept late and didn't go to church at all. For non-Catholics, it seemed, there was all white and no yolk.

In twelve years of Catholic schooling, I learned, in fact, very little about the beliefs of non-Catholics, though the little I learned was conveyed by my teachers without hostility and with fair accuracy. All that I knew about Protestants was that they differed from Catholics. But what precisely distinguished a Baptist from a Methodist from an Episcopalian I could not have said. I surmised the clearest notion of Protestant theology from discussions of the Reformation. At that, Protestantism emerged only as deviance from Catholic practice and thought. Judaism was different. Before the Christian era Judaism was *my* religion, the nuns said. ('We are all Jews because of Christ.') But what happened to Judaism after Christ's death to the time the modern state of Israel was founded, I could not have said. Nor did I know a thing about Hinduism or Buddhism or Islam. I knew nothing about modern secular ideologies. In civics class a great deal was said about oppressive Soviet policies; but at no time did I hear classical Marxism explained. In church, at the close of mass, the congregation prayed for 'the conversion of Russia.'

It is not enough to say that I grew up a ghetto Catholic. As a Catholic schoolboy, I was educated a middle-class American. Even while grammar school nuns reminded me of my spiritual separateness from non-Catholics, they provided excellent *public* schooling. A school day began with prayer – the Morning Offering. Then there was the Pledge of Allegiance to the American flag. Religion class followed immediately. But afterward, for the rest of the day, I was taught well those skills of numbers and words crucial to my Americanization. Soon I became as Americanized as my classmates – most of whom were two or three generations removed from their immigrant ancestors, and all of whom were children of middle-class parents.

When we were eleven years old, the nuns would warn us about the dangers of mixed marriage (between a Catholic and a non-Catholic). And we heard a priest say that it was a mortal sin to read newspaper accounts of a Billy Graham sermon. But the ghetto Catholic Church, so defensive, so fearful of contact with non-Catholics, was already outdated when I entered the classroom. My classmates and I were destined to live in a world very different from that which the nuns remembered in Ireland or my parents remembered in Mexico. We were destined to live on unhallowed ground, beyond the gated city of God.

I was in high school when Kennedy's picture went up on the wall. And I remember feeling that he was 'one of us.' His election to the presidency, however, did not surprise me as it did my father. Nor was I encouraged by it. I did not take it as evidence that Catholics could, after all, participate fully in American public life. (I assumed that to be true.) When I was a senior in high school, consequently, I did not hesitate to apply to secular colleges.

It was to be in college, at Stanford, that my religious faith would seem to me suddenly pared. I would remain a Catholic, but a Catholic defined by a non-Catholic world. This is how I think of myself now. I remember my early Catholic schooling and recall an experience of religion very different from anything I have known since. Never since have I felt so much at home in the Church, so easy at mass. My grammar school years especially were the years when the great Church doors opened to enclose me, filling my day as I was certain the Church filled all time. Living in a community of shared faith, I enjoyed much more than mere social reenforcement of religious belief. Experienced continuously in public and private, Catholicism shaped my whole day. It framed my experience of eating and sleeping and washing; it named the season and the hour.

The sky was full then and the coming of spring was a religious event. I would awaken to the sound of garage doors creaking open and know without thinking that it was Friday and that my father was on his way to six-thirty mass. I saw, without bothering to notice, statues at home and at school of the Virgin and of Christ. I would write at the top of my arithmetic or history homework the initials *Jesus*, *Mary*, and *Joseph*. (All my homework was thus dedicated.) I felt the air was different, somehow still and more silent on Sundays and high feastdays. I felt lightened, transparent as sky, after confessing my sins to a priest. Schooldays were routinely divided by prayers said with classmates. I would not have forgotten to say grace before eating. And I would not have turned off the light next to my bed or fallen asleep without praying to God.

I

The institution of the Church stood an extraordinarily physical presence in my world. One block from the house was
Sacred Heart Church. In the opposite direction, another block
away, was Sacred Heart Grammar School, run by the Sisters of
Mercy. And from our backyard, I could see Mercy Hospital,
Sacramento's only Catholic hospital. All day I would hear the
sirens of death. Well before I was a student myself, I would
watch the Catholic school kids walk by the front of the house,
dressed in gray and red uniforms. From the front lawn I could
see people on the steps of the church, coming out, dressed in
black after funerals, or standing, the ladies in bright-colored
dresses in front of the church after a wedding. When I first
went to stores on errands for my mother, I could be seen by the
golden-red statue of Christ, where it hovered over the main
door of the church.

I was *un católico* before I was a Catholic. That is, I acquired
my earliest sense of the Church – and my membership in it –
through my parents' Mexican Catholicism. It was in Spanish
that I first learned to pray. I recited family prayers – not from
any book. And in those years when we felt alienated from *los
gringos*, my family went across town every week to the wooden
church of Our Lady of Guadalupe, which was decorated with
yellow Christmas tree lights all year long.

Very early, however, the *gringo* church in our neighborhood began to superimpose itself on our family life. The first
English-speaking dinner guest at our house was a priest from
Sacred Heart Church. I was about four years old at the time,
so I retain only random details with which to remember the
evening. But the visit was too important an event for me to
forget. I remember how my mother dressed her four children

in outfits it had taken her weeks to sew. I wore a white shirt and blue woolen shorts. (It was the first time I had been dressed up for a stranger.) I remember hearing the priest's English laughter. (It was the first time I had heard such sounds in the house.) I remember that my mother served a *gringo* meat loaf and that I was too nervous or shy to look up more than two or three times to study the priest's jiggling layers of face. (Smoothly, he made believe that there was conversation.) After dinner we all went to the front room where the priest took a small book from his jacket to recite some prayers, consecrating our house and our family. He left a large picture of a sad-eyed Christ, exposing his punctured heart. (A caption below records the date of his visit and the imprimatur of Francis Cardinal Spellman.) That picture survives. Hanging prominently over the radio or, later, the television set in the front room, it has retained a position of prominence in all the houses my parents have lived in since. It has been one of the few permanent fixtures in the environment of my life. Visitors to our house doubtlessly noticed it when they entered the door – saw it immediately as the sign we were Catholics. But I saw the picture too often to pay it much heed.

I saw a picture of the Sacred Heart in the grammar school classroom I entered two years after the priest's visit. The picture drew an important continuity between home and the classroom. When all else was different for me (as a scholarship boy) between the two worlds of my life, the Church provided an essential link. During my first months in school, I remember being struck by the fact that – although they worshipped in English – the nuns and my classmates shared my family's religion. The *gringos* were, in some way, like me, *católicos*. Gradually, however, with my assimilation in the schoolroom, I began to think of myself and my family as Catholics. The distinction blurred. At home and in class I heard about sin and Christ and Satan and the consoling presence of Mary the Virgin. It became one Catholic faith for me.

Only now do I trouble to notice what intricate differences separated home Catholicism from classroom Catholicism. In school, religious instruction stressed that man was a sinner. Influenced, I suspect, by a bleak melancholic strain in Irish Catholicism, the nuns portrayed God as a judge. I was carefully taught the demands He placed upon me. In the third grade I could distinguish between venial and mortal sin. I knew – and was terrified to know – that there was one unforgivable sin (against the Holy Ghost): the sin of despair. I knew the crucial distinction between perfect and imperfect contrition. I could distinguish sins of commission from sins of omission. And I learned how important it was to be in a state of grace at the moment of death.

Death. (How much nearer it seemed to the boy than it seems to me now.) Again and again the nuns would pull out the old stories of death-bed conversions; of Roman martyrdoms; of murdered African missionaries; of pious children dying of cancer to become tiny saints; of souls going immediately to heaven. We were taught how to baptize in case of emergency. I knew why some souls went to Limbo after the death of the body, and others went for a time to Purgatory, and why others went to heaven or hell – 'forever and ever.'

Among the assortment of possible sins to commit, sexual sins – the cherries – were certainly mentioned. With the first years of puberty, the last years of grammar school, we began hearing about 'sins of the flesh.' There were those special mornings when the priest would come over from church to take the boys to the cafeteria, while the nun remained with the girls – 'the young ladies' – in the classroom. For fifty minutes the priest would talk about the dangers of masturbation or petting, and some friend of mine would turn carefully in his chair to smirk in my direction or somebody else would jab me in the back with a pencil.

Unlike others who have described their Catholic schooling, I do not remember the nuns or the priests to have been obsessed with sexual sins. Perhaps that says more about me or my Mexican Catholicism than it says about what actually went on in the classroom. I remember, in any case, that I would sometimes hear with irony warnings about sins of the flesh. When we were in eighth grade the priest told us how dangerous it was to look at our naked bodies, even while taking a bath – and I noticed that he made the remark directly under a near-naked figure of Christ on the cross.

The Church, in fact, excited more sexual wonderment than it repressed. I regarded with awe the 'wedding ring' on a nun's finger, her black 'wedding veil' – symbols of marriage to God. I would study pictures of martyrs – white-robed virgins fallen in death and the young, almost smiling, St. Sebastian, transfigured in pain. At Easter high mass I was dizzied by the mucous perfume of white flowers at the celebration of rebirth. At such moments, the Church touched alive some very private sexual excitement; it pronounced my sexuality important.

Sin remained, nevertheless. Confession was a regular part of my grammar school years. (One sought forgiveness through the ritual plea: 'Bless me, father, for I have sinned. . . .') Sin – the distance separating man from God – sin that burdened a sorrowful Christ; sin remained. ('I have disobeyed my parents fourteen times . . . I have lied eight times . . . I am heartily sorry for having offended Thee. . . .') God the Father judged. But Christ the Son had interceded. I was forgiven each time I sought forgiveness. The priest murmured Latin words of forgiveness in the confessional box. And I would leave the dark.

In contrast to the Catholicism of school, the Mexican Catholicism of home was less concerned with man the sinner than with man the supplicant. God the Father was not so much a stern judge as One with the power to change our lives. My family turned to God not in guilt so much as in need. We prayed for favors and at desperate times. I prayed for help in finding a quarter I had lost on my way home. I prayed with my family at times of illness and when my father was temporarily out of a job. And when there was death in the family, we prayed.

I remember my family's religion, and I hear the whispering voices of women. For although men in my family went to church, women prayed most audibly. Whether by man or woman, however, God the Father was rarely addressed directly. There were intermediaries to carry one's petition to Him. My mother had her group of Mexican and South American saints and near-saints (persons moving toward canonization). She favored a black Brazilian priest who, she claimed, was especially efficacious. Above all mediators there was Mary, *Santa María*, the Mother. Whereas at school the primary mediator was Christ, at home that role was assumed by the Mexican Virgin, *Nuestra Señora de Guadalupe*, the focus of devotion and pride for Mexican Catholics. The Mexican Mary 'honored our people,' my mother would say. 'She could have appeared to anyone in the whole world, but she appeared to a Mexican.' Someone like us. And she appeared, I could see from her picture, as a young Indian maiden – dark just like me.

On her feastday in early December my family would go to the Mexican church for a predawn high mass. The celebration would begin in the cold dark with a blare of trumpets imitating the cries of a cock. The Virgin's wavering statue on the shoulders of men would lead a procession into the warm yellow church. Often an usher would roughly separate me from my parents and pull me into a line of young children. (My mother nodded calmly when I looked back.) Sometimes alone, sometimes with my brother and sisters, I would find myself near the altar amid two or three hundred children, many of them dressed like Mexican cowboys and cowgirls. Sitting on the floor it was easier to see the congregation than the altar. So, as the mass progressed, my eye would wander through the crowd. Invariably, my attention settled on old women – mysterious supplicants in black – bent deep, their hands clasped tight to hold steady the attention of the Mexican Virgin, who was pictured high over the altar, astride a black moon.

The *gringo* Catholic church, a block from our house, was a very different place. In the *gringo* church Mary's statue was relegated to a side altar, imaged there as a serene white lady who matter-of-factly squashed the Genesis serpent with her bare feet. (Very early I knew that I was supposed to believe that the shy Mexican Mary was the same as this European Mary triumphant.) In the *gringo* church the floors were made not of squeaky wood but of marble. And there was not the devotional clutter of so many pictures and statues and candle racks. 'It doesn't feel like a church,' my mother complained. But as it became our regular church, I grew to love its elegant simplicity: the formal march of its eight black pillars toward the altar; the Easter-egg-shaped sanctuary that arched high over the tabernacle; and the dim pink light suffused throughout on summer afternoons when I came in not to pray but to marvel at the cool calm.

The holy darkness of church never frightened me. It was never nighttime darkness. Religion at school and at church was never nighttime religion like religion at home. Catholicism at home was shaped by the sounds of the 'family rosary': tired voices repeating the syllables of the Hail Mary; our fingers inching forward on beads toward the point of beginning; my knees aching; the coming of sleep.

Religion at home was a religion of bedtime. Prayers before sleeping spoke of death coming during the night. It was then a religion of shadows. The last thing I'd see before closing my eyes would be the cheap statue of Mary aglow next to my bed.

But the dark at the foot of my bed billowed with malevolent shapes. Those nights when I'd shudder awake from a nightmare, I'd remember my grandmother's instruction to make a sign of the cross in the direction of my window. (That way Satan would find his way barred.) Sitting up in bed, I'd aim the sign of the cross against the dim rectangle of light. Quickly, then, I'd say the Prayer to My Guardian Angel, which would enable me to fall back to sleep.

In time dawn came.

A child whose parents could not introduce him to books like *Grimm's Fairy Tales*, I was introduced to the spheres of enchantment by the nighttime Catholicism of demons and angels. The superstitious Catholicism of home provided a kind of proletarian fairy-tale world.

Satan was mentioned in the classroom. And depicted on the nuns' cartoon placards as bringing all his evil to bear on the temptation of nicely dressed boys and girls. In the morning's bright light and in the safe company of classmates, Satan never aroused very much terror. Around the time I was in fourth grade, moreover, religion classes became increasingly academic. I was introduced to that text familiar to generations of Catholic students, *The Baltimore Catechism.* It is a text organized by questions about the Catholic faith. (Who is God? What is Penance? What is Hope?)

Today's Catholic elementary schools attempt a less mechanical approach to religious instruction. Students are taught – what I never had to be taught – that religion is not simply a matter of dogmas or theological truths; that religion involves a person's whole way of life. To make the point, emphasis has shifted from the theological to the ethical. Students are encouraged to consider social problems and responses to 'practical' dilemmas in a modern world through which angels and devils no longer dance.

My schooling belonged to another time. *The Baltimore Catechism* taught me to trust the authority of the Church. That was the central lesson conveyed through the experience of memorizing hundreds of questions and answers. I learned an answer like, God made us to know, love, and serve Him in this life, and to be happy with Him in the next. The answer was memorized *along with* the question (it belonged with the question), Why did God make us? I learned, in other words, question and answer together. Beyond what the answer literally stated, two things were thus communicated. First, the existence of a question implies the existence of an answer. (There are no stray questions.) And second, that my questions about religion had answers. (The Church knows.)

Not only in religion class was memory exercised. During those years when I was memorizing the questions and answers of *The Baltimore Catechism*, I was also impressing on my memory the spelling of hundreds of words, grammar rules, division and multiplication tables. The nuns deeply trusted the role of memorization in learning. Not coincidentally, they were excellent teachers of basics. They would stand in front of the room for hours, drilling us over and over (5 times 5 . . . 5 times 9; *i* before *e* except after *c*; God made us to know, love, and serve Him in this world . . .). Stressing memorization, my teachers implied that education is largely a matter of acquiring knowledge already discovered. And they were right. For contrary to more progressive notions of learning, much that is learned in a classroom must be the already known; and much that is already known must be learned before a student can achieve truly independent thought.

Stressing memorization, the nuns assumed an important Catholic bias. Stated positively, they believed that learning is a social activity; learning is a rite of passage into the group. (Remembrance is itself an activity that establishes a student's dependence upon and union with others.) Less defensibly, the nuns distrusted intellectual challenges to authority. In religion class especially, they would grow impatient with the relentlessly questioning student. When one nun told my parents that their youngest daughter had a 'mind of her own,' she meant the remark to be a negative criticism. And even though I was urged to read all that I could, several teachers were dismayed to learn that I had read the novels of Victor Hugo and Flaubert. ('Those writers are on the Index, Richard.') With classmates I would hear the nuns' warning about non-Catholic colleges, stories of Faustian Catholics falling victim to the foolish sin of intellectual pride.

Trust the Church. It was the institution established by the instruction of Christ to his disciple: 'Thou art Peter and upon

this rock I will build. . . .' (How could Protestants not hear?)
The nun drew her pointer to the chart in front of the classroom
where the line of popes connected the name of St. Peter to that
of Pope Pius XII. Trust the Church, the nun said. It was
through the Church that God was best known. I came to believe: 'I am a Catholic.' (My faith in the Christian God was
enclosed by my faith in the Church.)

I never read the Bible alone. In fifth grade, when I told a
teacher that I intended to read the New Testament over the
summer, I did not get the praise I expected. Instead, the nun
looked worried and said I should delay my plan for a while.
('Wait until we read it in class.') In the seventh and eighth
grades, my class finally did read portions of the Bible. We read
together. And our readings were guided by the teachings of
Tradition – the continuous interpretation of the Word passing
through generations of Catholics. Thus, as a reader I never
forgot the ancient Catholic faith – that the Church serves to
help solitary man comprehend God's Word.

2

Of all the institutions in their lives, only the Catholic
Church has seemed aware of the fact that my mother and
father are thinkers – persons aware of the experience of their
lives. Other institutions – the nation's political parties, the in-
dustries of mass entertainment and communications, the com-
panies that employed them – have all treated my parents with
condescension. The Church too has treated them badly when it
attempted formal instruction. The homily at Sunday mass, intended to give parishioners basic religious instruction, has often
been poorly prepared and aimed at a childish listener. It has

been the liturgical Church that has excited my parents. In ceremonies of public worship, they have been moved, assured that
their lives – all aspects of their lives, from waking to eating,
from birth until death, all moments – possess great significance.
Only the liturgy has encouraged them to dwell on the meaning
of their lives. To think.

What the Church gave to my mother and father, it gave to
me. During those years when the nuns warned me about the
dangers of intellectual pride and referred to Christ as Baby
Jesus, they were enabling me to participate fully in the liturgical
life of the Church. The nuns were not interested in constructing
a temple of religious abstractions. God was more than an idea;
He was person – white-bearded, with big arms. (Pictures could
not show what He really was like, the nuns said, but one could
be sure that He was Our Father.) He loved us and we were to
respond, like children, in love. Our response would be prayer.

In my first-grade classroom I learned to make the sign of
the cross with English words. In addition to prayers said at
home (prayers before dinner and before sleeping), there were
prayers in the classroom. A school day was divided by prayer.
First, the Morning Offering. At 10:15, before recess, the Prayer
to My Guardian Angel. At noontime, the Angelus, in celebration of the Word: 'The angel of the Lord declared unto
Mary . . .' After lunch came the Creed. And before going
home the Act of Contrition. In first grade I was taught to make
the sign of the cross when I entered the church. And how to
genuflect (the right knee bending and touching all the way to
the floor). And the nuns told us of the most perfect prayer
(Christ's offering of His body and blood to the Father), the
'sacrifice' of the mass.

Alongside red, yellow, blue, green, Dick and Jane, was

disclosed to us the knowledge of our immortal souls. And that our souls (we were Catholics) needed the special nourishment of the Church – the mass and the sacraments.

In second grade, at the age of seven, we were considered by the Church to have reached the age of reason; we were supposed capable of distinguishing good from evil. We were able to sin; able to ask forgiveness for sin. In second grade, I was prepared for my first Confession, which took place on a Saturday morning in May. With all my classmates, I went to the unlit church where the nun led us through the forms of an 'examination of conscience.' Then, one by one – as we would be summoned to judgment after death – we entered the airless confessional. The next day – spotless souls – we walked as a class up the aisle of church, the girls in white dresses and veils like small brides, the boys in white pants and white shirts. We walked to the altar rail where the *idea* of God assumed a shape and a scent and a taste.

As an eight-year-old Catholic, I learned the names and functions of all seven sacraments. I knew why the priest put glistening oil on my grandmother's forehead the night she died. At the baptismal font I watched a baby cry out as the priest trickled a few drops of cold water on his tiny red forehead. At ten I knew the meaning of the many ritual gestures the priest makes during the mass. I knew (by heart) the drama of feast-days and seasons – and could read the significance of changing altar cloth colors as the year slowly rounded.

The Church rocked through time – a cradle, an ark – to rhythms of sorrow and joy, marking the passage of man.

The Catholic calendar in my bedroom was printed by W. F. Gormley and Sons, morticians. Every month there was a dif-

ferent Bible picture in beautiful colors. Every day was something. The calendar noted ferial and ember days, fish days and
the feastdays of saints. (My birthday honored St. Ignatius Loy-
ola.) There was another, a 'regular,' calendar in the kitchen
(Capitol Savings and Loan). It noted full moons and crescents
and the official change of the seasons. My mother used the
regular calendar to write down our doctors' appointments
(shots; teeth).

It was the religious calendar that governed my school year.
In early September there was a nine o'clock mass on the Friday
of the first week of school to pray for academic success. (Students were grouped according to class; behind my class would
be my new teacher's face, a face I still wasn't used to.) In June,
there was a mass of graduation for the eighth-graders. Between
those events, school often stopped or flowered as routine bowed
to the sacred. In the middle of a geography or an arithmetic
lesson, the nuns would lead us out of our classrooms and we
would walk – four hundred students in double lines – down a
block to church, stopping traffic (We were Catholics!) to attend
a First Friday mass or a rosary to Mary. In Lent there were
Friday Stations of the Cross. (Fourteen meditations on the
passion of Christ – He stumbled, He fell – fourteen times the
priest intoning, 'We adore Thee, O Christ. . . .') Benediction,
the adoration of the Host, followed. The lovely hymn, the
Tantum Ergo sounded as smoke of incense rose like vine. Upon
the high altar stood a golden monstrance in the shape of a sun-
burst, at the center of which – exposed through a tiny window
– was the round wafer of bread. We returned to the classroom,
came back to the same paragraph in a still-opened book. Routine resumed. Sacred dramas of Church thus fitted into a day,
never became the routine; rather they redeemed the routine.

On Halloween night, all over Sacramento, children dressed up as ghosts or Frankensteins or dime-store skeletons with phosphorescent bones. But only Catholic school kids went to mass the next morning to honor the white-robed saints on the Feast of All Hallows. It was one of the 'holy days of obligation' – a day on which I was obliged to go to morning mass, but for the rest of the day I was free – no school. I could ride my bicycle around Sacramento; watch public school kids walking to school. And people downtown were passing just another day. (They seemed not to know.)

In the secular calendar there was no day like Ash Wednesday. All day I would see on the heedless foreheads of classmates the Hindu-like smudge of dark ash, the reminder of death. (. . . Unto dust thou shalt return.) One year a girl at school was killed in a car crash shortly after Ash Wednesday. I took the lesson.

On those few occasions when secular Sacramento took up the sacred calendar they got it all wrong. Christmas downtown began in early November. Merchants would string tiny white lights up over K Street, where they shone through the night as pretty as heaven. But their Christmas ended in late afternoon on Christmas Eve – I saw department store clerks working against time to replace a holiday window display with deathly white piles of towels and sheets. In church, in early November there was Advent, the time for penance. On a table in front of the altar was a wreath with four candles stuck in, one of which was lit each week to mark the coming – the slow, slow coming – of Christ. In church, Christmas began at midnight mass, Christmas Eve. And the holy season continued until the Feast of Epiphany, the sixth of January, when carols were sung for the very last time and fir trees on the altar no longer cast their dark scent of damp earth.

The secular calendar whirled like a carnival wheel and offered carnival prizes – a fat Santa instead of the infant God; colored eggs and chocolate bunnies instead of the death and resurrection of Christ. During Holy Week all pictures and statues in church were shrouded by purple silk drapes. On Holy Thursday to commemorate the Last Supper of Christ there was a 'white' mass at sunset (when stained-glass windows burned briefly before the light failed). After that mass, the sacrament was removed to a side altar and the red sanctuary lamp was extinguished, so that the next day, Good Friday, when women in scarves and men in work clothes came to church for 'the three hours' they found an altar stripped bare and the tabernacle gaping.

In our house on Good Friday we behaved as if a member of our family had died. There was no radio or television. But I noticed that the Standard gas station right across from church stayed open for business as usual and I saw people at the Laundromat watching their clothes tumble behind a round window – as if nothing in the world had happened. In Sacramento, the blue Easter morning seemed always to rhyme with the gospel account of the three Marys wending their way through a garden to discover an empty tomb. At church, at the altar, there were vestments of gold and the climbing voices of a Mozart mass, tossing rings sempiternal.

The wheels turned. Two wheels of time. The secular calendar made plain note of the hot first day of summer. Fall. Then winter. Ordinary time: Labor Day. The first day of school. Arithmetic class. An hour for spelling (a test every Friday). Recess. Church time: Benediction with classmates. Candles on St. Blaise's day. Ash. Palms in April. The red-eyed white dove descending, descending on Pentecost Sunday. Mary crowned with dying sweet flowers on the first day of May. The wheels turned. Second grade. Third grade. Fifth grade. Christmas. Epiphany. The secular calendar announced the vernal equinox. The low valley fog of late winter would slowly yield to the coming of Easter.

I went to the nine o'clock mass every Sunday with my family. At that time in my life, when I was so struck by diminished family closeness and the necessity of public life, church was a place unlike any other. It mediated between my public and private lives. I would kneel beside my brother and sisters. On one side of us would be my mother. (I could hear her whispered Spanish Hail Mary.) On the other side, my father. In the pew directly in front of us were the Van Hoyts. And in front of them were the druggist and his family. Over to the side was a lady who wore fancy dresses, a widow who prayed a crystal rosary. She was alone, as was the old man in front who cupped his face in his hands while he prayed. It was this same gesture of privacy the nuns would teach me to use, especially after Communion when I thanked God for coming into my soul.

The mass mystified me for being a public and a private event. We prayed here, each of us, much as we prayed on our pillows – most privately – all alone before God. And yet the great public prayer of the mass would go on. No one ever forgot where they were. People stood up together or they knelt at the right time in response to the progression of the liturgy. Every Sunday in summer someone fainted from heat, had to be carried out, but the mass went on.

I remember being puzzled very early by how different things were for the Protestants. Evangelical Christians would ring the doorbell to ask bluntly whether or not I was 'saved.' They proceeded to tell me about their own conversions to

Christ. From classmates I would hear about Holy Rollers who jumped up and down and even fell to the floor at their services. It was funny. Hard to believe. My religion – the true religion – was so different. On Sunday afternoons, for a guilty few minutes, I'd watch an Oral Roberts prayer meeting on television. Members of the congregation made public confessions of sin, while people off camera shouted, 'Hallelujah, sister! Hallelujah, brother, preach it!'

Sister and *Brother* were terms I used in speaking to my teachers for twelve years. *Father* was the name for the priest at church. I never confused my teachers or the priests with actual family members; in fact they were most awesome for being without families. Yet I came to use these terms with ease. They implied that a deep bond existed between my teachers and me as fellow Catholics. At the same time, however, *Sister* and *Father* were highly formal terms of address – they were titles, marks of formality like a salute or a curtsey. (One would never have spoken to a nun without first calling her Sister.) It was possible consequently to use these terms and to feel at once a close bond, and the distance of formality. In a way, that is how I felt with all fellow Catholics in my world. We were close – somehow related – while also distanced by careful reserve.

Not once in all the years of my Catholic schooling did I hear a classmate or teacher make a public confession. ('Public' confessions were whispered through darkness to the shadow of a priest sworn to secrecy.) Never once did I hear a classmate or teacher make an exclamation of religious joy. Religious feelings and faith were channeled through ritual. Thus it was that my classmates and I prayed easily throughout the school day. We recited sublime prayers and childish ones ('Angel of

God, my guardian dear . . .'). And nobody snickered. Because the prayers were always the same and because they were said by the group, we had a way of praying together without being self-conscious.

Children of ceremony: My classmates and I would rehearse our roles before major liturgical celebrations. Several days before a feastday we would learn the movements for a procession. In the half-darkened church one nun stood aside with a wooden clapper which she knocked to tell us when to rise, when to kneel, when to leave the pew, when to genuflect ('All together!'). We'd rehearse marching (the tallest last) up the aisle in straight, careful lines. Worship was managed as ceremony.

My sense of belonging in this ceremonial Church was dearest when I turned twelve and became an altar boy. Dressed in a cassock like a priest's I assisted at the performance of mass on the altar. It was my responsibility to carry the heavy red missal back and forth from one side of the altar to the other; to pour water and sweet-scented wine into the priest's chalice; to alert the congregation with a handbell at the *Sanctus* and at the elevation of the Host. But by far the greatest responsibility was to respond to the priest in memorized Latin prayers. I served as the voice of the congregation, sounding, all told, perhaps a hundred responsorial lines.

Latin, the nuns taught us, was a universal language. One could go into a Catholic church anywhere in the world and hear the very same mass. But Latin was also a dead language, a tongue foreign to most Catholics. As an altar boy, I memorized Latin in blank envelopes of sound: *Ad day um qui lay tee fee cat u ven tu tem may um.* Many of the 'ordinary' prayers of the mass were generally recognizable to me. (Any Catholic who used a bilingual missal could, after a while, recognize the meaning of whole prayers like the *Credo*.) I had the advantage of being able to hear in the shrouded gallery of Latin sounds echoes of Spanish words familiar to me. Listening to a priest I could often grasp the general sense of what he was saying – but I didn't always try to. In part, Latin permitted escape from the prosaic world. Latin's great theatrical charm, its sacred power, was that it could translate human aspiration to a holy tongue. The Latin mass, moreover, encouraged private reflection. The sounds of Latin would sometimes blur my attention to induce an aimless drift inward. But then I would be called back by the priest's voice (*'Oremus . . .'*) to public prayer, the reminder that an individual has the aid of the Church in his life. I was relieved of the burden of being alone before God through my membership in the Church.

Parish priests recognized and encouraged my fascination with the liturgy. During the last three years of grammar school, I was regularly asked to 'serve' as an altar boy. In my busiest year, eighth grade, I served at over two hundred masses. I must have served at about thirty baptisms and about the same number of weddings and funerals. During the school year I was excused from class for an hour or two to serve at a funeral mass. In summertime I would abandon adolescence to put the black cassock of mourning over a light summer shirt. A spectator at so many funerals, I grew acquainted with the rhythms of grief. I knew at which moments, at which prayers in church and at gravesides, survivors were most likely to weep. I studied faces. I learned to trust the grief of persons who showed no emotion. With the finesse of a mortician, I would lead mourners to the grave. I helped carry coffins (their mysterious weight – neither heavy nor light) to burial sites when there were not mourners enough. And then I would return. To class or to summer. Resume my life as a boy of thirteen.

There are people who tell me today that they are not religious because they consider religion to be an evasion of life. I hear them, their assurance, and do not bother to challenge the arrogance of a secular world which hasn't courage enough to accept the fact of old age. And death. I know people who speak of death with timorous euphemisms of 'passing away.' I have friends who wouldn't think of allowing their children to attend a funeral for fear of inflicting traumatic scars. For my part, I will always be grateful to the Church that took me so seriously and exposed me so early, through the liturgy, to the experience of life. I will always be grateful to the parish priest who forced a mortician to remove an elaborate arrangement of flowers from a coffin: 'Don't hide it!'

I celebrate now a childhood lived through the forms of the liturgical Church. As the Church filled my life, I grew to the assurance that my life, my every action and thought, was important for good or for bad. Bread and wine, water, oil, salt, and ash – through ceremonies of guilt and redemption, sorrow and rebirth, through the passing liturgical year, my boyhood assumed all significance. I marvel most at having so easily prayed with others – not simply alone. I recall standing at the altar at Easter, amid candles and gold vestments, hearing the Mozart high mass. These were impossible riches. I remember wanting to cry out with joy, to shout. I wanted to shout. But I didn't, of course. I worshipped in a ceremonial church, one in a group. I remained silent and remembered to genuflect exactly on cue. After the mass, I pulled off the surplice and cassock and rushed to meet my parents, waiting for me in front of the church. 'It was very nice today,' my mother said. Something like that. 'It makes you feel good, the beautiful music and everything.' That was all that she said. It was enough.

3

Now. I go to mass every Sunday. Old habits persist. But it is an English mass I attend, a ritual of words. A ritual that seeks to feed my mind and would starve my somewhat metaphorical soul. The mass is less ornamental; it has been 'modernized,' tampered with, demythologized, deflated. The priest performs fewer gestures. His central role as priest – intermediary between congregation and God – is diminished. Symbols have changed. A reciprocal relationship between people and clergy is dramatized as the congregation takes an active role in the recitation of the mass. The priest faces the people, his back to the tabernacle. And the effect of this rearrangement is to make the mass seem less a prayer directed to God, more a communal celebration of the Eucharist. There is something occasional about it all, and no occasion for pomp or solemnity. No longer is the congregation moved to a contemplation of the timeless. Rather it is the idiomatic one hears. One's focus is upon this place. This time. The moment. Now.

In the old Latin mass my mother could recite her rosary while still being at one with prayer at the altar. The new English mass is unilinear, lacking density; there is little opportunity for private prayer. The English words enforce attention. Emphasis is on the communal prayer, communal identity. There is a moment just before the Communion when members of the congregation shake hands to dramatize a union. We nod and bow, shake hands like figures on a music box.

I go along with the Kiss of Peace, but paradoxically I feel isolated sitting in half-empty churches among people I am suddenly aware of not knowing. The kiss signifies to me a betrayal of the older ceremonial liturgy. I miss that high ceremony. I am saddened by inappropriate music about which it is damning enough to say that it is not good enough, and not even the best of its authentic kind – folk, pop, quasi-religious Broadway show tunes. I miss the old trappings – trappings that disclosed a different reality. I have left church early, walked out, after hearing the congregation spontaneously applaud its own singing. And I have wondered how the Church I loved could have changed so quickly and completely.

I continue to claim my Catholicism. Invariably I arrive late at somebody's brunch or tennis party – the festivities of a secular Sunday. Friends find it peculiar that I still go to mass; most have heard me complain about liturgical changes. Amid the orange juice and croissants I burlesque the folk-mass liturgy ('Kumbaya'), the peppy tambourine. Those listening find my sarcasm amusing. And someone says that my Catholicism is a mere affectation, an attempt to play the Evelyn Waugh eccentric to a bland and vulgar secular age.

I am not surprised. I do not know myself, not with any certainty, how much I really am saying when I profess Catholicism. In a cultural sense, I remain a Catholic. My upbringing has shaped in me certain attitudes which have not worn thin over the years. I am, for example, a materialist largely because I was brought up to believe in the central mystery of the Church – the redemptive Incarnation. (I carried the heavy gold crucifix in church ceremonies far too often to share the distrust of the material still prevalent in modern Puritan America.) I am a man who trusts a society that is carefully ordered by figures of authority. (I respond to policemen in the same tone of voice I used years ago, addressing parish priests and nuns.) I realize that I am a Catholic, moreover, when I listen skeptically to a political thinker describe with enthusiasm a scheme for lasting political change. (My historical pessimism was determined by grammar school lessons about sin, especially Original Sin.)

More important than any of this, I continue to believe the central tenets of the Church. I stand at the Creed of the mass. Though it is exactly then, at that very moment in the liturgy, when I must realize how different the Church has become in recent years. I stand as a stranger among strangers. For the truth is: It is not only the Church that has changed; I've changed as well.

My Catholicism changed when I was in high school. The liturgy was just then beginning to be altered. It was not simply that I found a different Church when I went to church; I went to church less often. (My high school was not connected to a neighborhood church the way my grammar school had been. There were, consequently, few schooldays interrupted by worship.) Liturgy was something for Sunday.

My high school, staffed by the Christian Brothers, offered a more 'Protestant' education. My freshman literature teacher only smiled when I mentioned the grammar school incident concerning Flaubert. He and other high school teachers encouraged my intellectual independence. Religious instruction became rigorously intellectual. With excitement I'd study complex Pauline and Thomistic theology and I'd remember with something like scorn the simple instructions of *The Baltimore Catechism*. In high school I started saying that I *believed* in Catholicism. My faith was buttressed by a book by Jacques Maritain rather than by the experience of worship at a Lenten service with classmates or serving at some old lady's funeral. Those years were marked by the realization that my parents assumed a Catholicism very different from mine. My parents seemed to me piously simple – like the nuns I remembered –

unwilling to entertain intellectual challenges. They would rely on their rosary every night, while in another room I read patristic theology.

In college I had few Catholic friends and fewer Catholic teachers. Most of my friends had been raised as Protestants or Jews; many referred to themselves as agnostics. During my college years I started reading Protestant theology. The Church was no longer my sole spiritual teacher. I blended Catholicism with borrowed insights from Sartre and Zen and Buber and Miltonic Protestantism. And Freud.

I was a senior at Stanford during the last year of the Vatican Council. I cheered for the liberal bishops and cardinals at that great convocation. (The villains, in my view, were the conservatives of the Roman Curia.) I welcomed the Church's attempts at reconciliation with other religions. I approved of the liberal encyclicals concerning 'the Church in the modern world.' But I was changing rather more quickly than the Council fathers were changing the Church. I was already a 'new Catholic.' I didn't wait for the American bishops to terminate the observance of meatless Fridays before I ate what looked best in the dormitory cafeteria on Friday nights. Nor did I request a dispensation from a priest when a non-Catholic friend asked me to be his best man. I simply agreed and stood beside him in a Methodist church.

I would go to friends for advice when I was troubled; I didn't go to priests anymore. I stopped going to Confession, not because my behavior conflicted with the teachings of the institutional Church but because I no longer thought to assess my behavior against those standards. A Catholic who lived most of his week without a sense of communal Catholicism, I relied upon conscience as never before. The priest who was the college chaplain would regularly say in his sermons that a Catholic must rely upon conscience as his ultimate guide. It seemed so to me. But I remember feeling uneasy when that priest was later excommunicated for having been secretly married.

Throughout college and graduate school, I thought of myself as an orthodox Catholic. I was a liberal Catholic. In all things save the liturgy I was a liberal. From the start I despised the liturgical reformation. In college chapels I would listen to folk singing and see plain altars draped with bright appliqué banners: JOY! GOD IS LOVE. One Sunday I would watch dancers in leotards perform some kind of ballet in front of the altar; one Sunday there would be a rock mass; one Sunday the priest encouraged us to spend several minutes before the Offertory introducing ourselves, while a small bad jazzy combo punched out a cocktail mix. I longed for the Latin mass. Incense. Music of Bach. Ceremonies of candles and acolytes.

Over the last several years, I have visited many Catholic churches in the several cities I have lived in. Palo Alto. New York. Berkeley. Los Angeles. London. San Francisco. I have wandered on Sundays from church to church. But in all the churches I have had to listen to the new English mass. The proclamation of faith, the Creed, I hear recited by the congregation around me. 'We believe in God. . . .' In the abandoned Latin service it was the priest alone who spoke the affirmation of faith. It was the priest who said, '*Credo* . . . ,' using the first person singular. The differences between the old service and the new can be summarized in this change. At the old mass, the priest's *Credo* (I believe) complexly reminded the congregation of the fact that each person stands before God as an individual, implying at the same time – because the priest could join all voices in his – the union of believers, the consolation of communal faith. The listener was assured of his membership in the Church; he was not alone before God. (The Church would assist him.) By translating *credo* into the English first person plural, *we* believe, the Church no longer reminds the listener that he is alone. 'We believe,' the congregation is encouraged to say, celebrating community – but only that fact.

I would protest this simplification of the liturgy if I could. I would protest as well the diminished sense of the sacred in churches today. I would protest the use of folk music and the hand-holding. Finally, I cannot. I suspect that the reason I despise the new liturgy is because it is mine. It reflects and attempts to resolve the dilemma of Catholics just like me. The informal touches; the handshaking; the folk music; the insistence upon union – all these changes are aimed at serving Catholics who no longer live in a Catholic world. To such Catholics – increasingly alone in their faith – the Church says: You are part of a community of believers. You are not single in your faith. Not solitary. We are together, Catholics. *We* believe. We believe. We believe. This assurance is necessary because, in a sense, it no longer is true.

The Catholic Church of my past required no such obvious reminders of community as smiles and handshakes before the Communion. The old mass proceeded with sure, blind pomp precisely because Catholics had faith in their public identity as Catholics; the old liturgy was ceremonial because of the Church's assumption that worship is a public event. The lack of high ceremony in church today betrays a loss of faith in communal Catholicism. In obvious ways everyone in the congregation seems closer and more aware of each other. As a group, throughout mass, the congregation responds to the priest with various prayers; one listens to a steady flow of prayers said in English. But there is scant opportunity for private prayer. The Church cannot dare it.

A priest I once heard in a white middle-class parish defended the reformed liturgy by saying that it had become necessary to 'de-Europeanize' the Roman Catholic Church. He said that Catholicism must translate God's Word into the many languages and cultures of the world. I suppose he is right. I do not think, however, that the primary impetus for liturgical reformation came from Third World Catholics. I think rather that it came in response to a middle-class crisis of faith in North America and Western Europe. The new liturgy is suited especially to those who live in the secular city, alone in their faith for most of the week. It is not a liturgy suited to my parents or grandparents as much as to me.

When I go to church on Sunday I am forced to recognize a great deal about myself. I would rather go to a high ceremonial mass, reap for an hour or two its communal assurance. The sentimental solution would be ideal: to remain a liberal Catholic and to worship at a traditional mass. But now that I no longer live as a Catholic in a Catholic world, I cannot expect the liturgy – which reflects and cultivates my faith – to remain what it was. I will continue to go to the English mass. I will go because it is my liturgy. I will, however, often recall with nostalgia the faith I have lost. And I will be uneasy knowing that the old faith was lost as much by *choice* as it was inevitably lost. My education may have made it inevitable that I would become a citizen of the secular city, but I have come to *embrace* the city's values: social mobility; pluralism; egalitarianism; self-reliance. By choice I do not confine myself to Catholic society. Most of my friends and nearly all of my intimates are non-

Catholics. With them I normally will observe the politesse of secular society concerning religion – say nothing about it. By choice I do not pray before eating lunch in a downtown restaurant. (My public day is not divided by prayer.) By choice I do not consult the movie ratings of the Legion of Decency, and my reading is not curtailed by the Index. By choice I am ruled by conscience rather than the authority of priests I consider my equals. I do not listen to papal pronouncements with which I disagree.

Recently, bishops and popes who have encouraged liturgical reforms have seemed surprised at the insistence of so many Catholics to determine for themselves the morality of such matters as divorce, homosexuality, contraception, abortion, and extramarital sex. But the Church fathers who initiated rituals that reflect a shared priesthood of laity and clergy should not be surprised by the independence of modern Catholics. The authoritarian Church belonged to another time. It was an upper-class Church; it was a lower-class Church. It was a hierarchical Church. It was my grandparents' Church.

If I ask questions about religion that my grandparents didn't ask, it is not because I am intellectually advanced. I wonder about the existence of God because, unlike my grandparents, I live much of my day in a secular city where I do not measure the hours with the tolling bells of a church. As a boy, I believed in God by believing in His Church. Now that my faith in communal Catholicism is so changed, my faith in God is without certain foundation. It occurs to me to ask that profound question of modern agnosticism: Is God dead?

I would cry into the void. . . . If I should lose my faith in God, I would have no place to go to where I could feel myself a man. The Catholic Church of my youth mediated with special grace between the public and private realms of my life, such was the extent of its faith in itself. That Church is no longer mine. I cling to the new Catholic Church. Though it leaves me unsatisfied, I fear giving it up, falling through space. Even in today's Catholic Church, it is possible for me to feel myself in the eye of God, while I kneel in the presence of others.

If God is dead, where shall I go for such an experience? In this modern post-religious age, secular institutions flounder to imitate the gift that is uniquely found in the temple and mosque and church. Secular institutions lack the key; they have no basis for claiming access to the realm of the private. When they try to deny their limits, secular institutions only lie. They pretend that there is no difference between public and private life. The worst are totalitarian governments. They respect no notion of privacy. They intrude into a family's life. They ignore the individual's right to be private. They would bulldoze the barrier separating the public from the private. They create the modern nightmare of institutional life.

If God is dead I will cry into the void.

There was a time in my life when it would never have occurred to me to make a confession like this one. There was a time when I would never have thought to discuss my spiritual life – even with other Catholics I knew intimately. It is true that in high school I read Augustine's *Confessions*, but that extraordinary autobiography did not prompt my imitation. Just the reverse: There seemed to me something non-Catholic about the *Confessions*. I intuited that such revelations made Augustine a Protestant church father more than a Catholic father.

Years after, in college, I remember reading the diaries of seventeenth-century Puritans. To encounter 'simple' people – a tradesman, a housewife, a farmer – describing their spiritual lives in detail amazed me. The Protestant confession was boldly different from the Catholic sacrament of Confession. The Protestants were public about their spiritual lives in a way that I, as a Catholic schoolboy, could never have been. Protestants were so public because they were otherwise alone in their faith. I marveled at the paradox implied by their writings. Those early 'pure' English Protestants, strangers to ceremony, and for their own reasons alien from the institutional Church, were attempting to form through their writings a new kind of Christian community – a community of those who share with each other *only* the experience of standing alone before God. It was then that I began to realize the difference separating the individualistic Protestant from the institutional Catholic. Now I realize that I have become like a Protestant Christian. I call myself a Christian.

My own Catholic Church in recent years has become more like a Protestant Church. Perhaps Protestants will teach Catholics like me how to remain believers when the sense one has for so much of one's day is of being alone in faith. If, in fact, my spiritual fathers are those seventeenth-century Puritans, there is one important difference between their writings and mine. I am writing about my religious life, aware that most of my readers do not consider themselves religious. With them – with you – I am making this admission of faith. It is appropriate that I do so. The resolution of my spiritual dilemma, if there is to be one before death, will have to take place where it began, among persons who do not share my religious convictions. Persons like my good friends now, those who, smiling, wonder why I am more than an hour late for their Sunday brunch.

FOUR

Complexion

Visiting the East Coast or the gray capitals of Europe during the long months of winter, I often meet people at deluxe hotels who comment on my complexion. (In such hotels it appears nowadays a mark of leisure and wealth to have a complexion like mine.) Have I been skiing? In the Swiss Alps? Have I just returned from a Caribbean vacation? No. I say no softly but in a firm voice that intends to explain: My complexion is dark. (My skin is brown. More exactly, terra-cotta in sunlight, tawny in shade. I do not redden in sunlight. Instead, my skin becomes progressively dark; the sun singes the flesh.)

When I was a boy the white summer sun of Sacramento would darken me so, my T-shirt would seem bleached against my slender dark arms. My mother would see me come up the front steps. She'd wait for the screen door to slam at my back. 'You look like a *negrito*,' she'd say, angry, sorry to be angry, frustrated almost to laughing, scorn. 'You know how important looks are in this country. With *los gringos* looks are all that they judge on. But you! Look at you! You're so careless!' Then she'd start in all over again. 'You won't be satisfied till you end up looking like *los pobres* who work in the fields, *los braceros*.'

(*Los braceros*: Those men who work with their *brazos*, their arms; Mexican nationals who were licensed to work for American farmers in the 1950s. They worked very hard for very little money, my father would tell me. And what money they earned they sent back to Mexico to support their families, my mother would add. *Los pobres* – the poor, the pitiful, the powerless ones. But paradoxically also powerful men. They were the men with brown-muscled arms I stared at in awe on Saturday mornings when they showed up downtown like gypsies to shop at Woolworth's or Penney's. On Monday nights they would gather hours early on the steps of the Memorial Auditorium for the wrestling matches. Passing by on my bicycle in summer, I would spy them there, clustered in small groups, talking – frightening and fascinating men – some wearing Texas *sombreros* and T-shirts which shone fluorescent in the twilight. I would sit forward in the back seat of our family's '48 Chevy to see them, working alongside Valley highways: dark men on an even horizon, loading a truck amid rows of straight green. Powerful, powerless men. Their fascinating darkness – like mine – to be feared.)

'You'll end up looking just like them.'

I

Regarding my family, I see faces that do not closely resemble my own. Like some other Mexican families, my family suggests Mexico's confused colonial past. Gathered around a table, we appear to be from separate continents. My father's face recalls faces I have seen in France. His complexion is white – he does not tan; he does not burn. Over the years, his dark wavy hair has grayed handsomely. But with time his face has sagged to a perpetual sigh. My mother, whose surname is inexplicably Irish – Moran – has an olive complexion. People have frequently wondered if, perhaps, she is Italian or Portuguese. And, in fact, she looks as though she could be from southern Europe. My mother's face has not aged as quickly as the rest of her body; it remains smooth and glowing – a cool tan – which her gray hair cleanly accentuates. My older brother has inherited her good looks. When he was a boy people would tell him that he looked like Mario Lanza, and hearing it he would smile with dimpled assurance. He would come home from high school with girl friends who seemed to me glamorous (because they were) blonds. And during those years I envied him his skin that burned red and peeled like the skin of the *gringos*. His complexion never darkened like mine. My youngest sister is exotically pale, almost ashen. She is delicately featured, Near Eastern, people have said. Only my older sister has a complexion as dark as mine, though her facial features are much less harshly defined than my own. To many people meeting her, she seems (they say) Polynesian. I am the only one in the family whose face is severely cut to the line of ancient Indian ancestors. My face is mournfully long, in the classical Indian manner; my profile suggests one of those beak-nosed Mayan sculptures – the eaglelike face upturned, open-mouthed, against the deserted, primitive sky.

'We are Mexicans,' my mother and father would say, and taught their four children to say whenever we (often) were asked about our ancestry. My mother and father scorned those 'white' Mexican-Americans who tried to pass themselves off as Spanish. My parents would never have thought of denying their ancestry. I never denied it: My ancestry is Mexican, I told strangers mechanically. But I never forgot that only my older sister's complexion was as dark as mine.

My older sister never spoke to me about her complexion when she was a girl. But I guessed that she found her dark skin a burden. I knew that she suffered for being a 'nigger.' As she came home from grammar school, little boys came up behind her and pushed her down to the sidewalk. In high school, she struggled in the adolescent competition for boyfriends in a world of football games and proms, a world where her looks were plainly uncommon. In college, she was afraid and scornful when dark-skinned foreign students from countries like Turkey and India found her attractive. She revealed her fear of dark skin to me only in adulthood when, regarding her own three children, she quietly admitted relief that they were all light.

That is the kind of remark women in my family have often made before. As a boy, I'd stay in the kitchen (never seeming to attract any notice), listening while my aunts spoke of their pleasure at having light children. (The men, some of whom were dark-skinned from years of working out of doors, would be in another part of the house.) It was the woman's spoken concern: the fear of having a dark-skinned son or daughter. Remedies were exchanged. One aunt prescribed to her sisters the elixir of large doses of castor oil during the last weeks of pregnancy. (The remedy risked an abortion.) Children born dark grew up to have their faces treated regularly with a mixture of egg white and lemon juice concentrate. (In my case, the solution never would take.) One Mexican-American friend of my mother's, who regarded it a special blessing that she had a measure of English blood, spoke disparagingly of her husband, a construction worker, for being so dark. 'He doesn't take care of himself,' she complained. But the remark, I noticed, annoyed my mother, who sat tracing an invisible design with her finger on the tablecloth.

There was affection too and a kind of humor about these matters. With daring tenderness, one of my uncles would refer to his wife as *mi negra*. An aunt regularly called her dark child *mi feito* (my little ugly one), her smile only partially hidden as she bent down to dig her mouth under his ticklish chin. And at times relatives spoke scornfully of pale, white skin. A *gringo's* skin resembled *masa* – baker's dough – someone remarked. Everyone laughed. Voices chuckled over the fact that the *gringos* spent so many hours in summer sunning themselves. ('They need to get sun because they look like *los muertos*.')

I heard the laughing but remembered what the women had said, with unsmiling voices, concerning dark skin. Nothing I heard outside the house, regarding my skin, was so impressive to me.

In public I occasionally heard racial slurs. Complete strangers would yell out at me. A teenager drove past, shouting, 'Hey, Greaser! Hey, Pancho!' Over his shoulder I saw the giggling face of his girl friend. A boy pedaled by and announced matter-of-factly, 'I pee on dirty Mexicans.' Such remarks would be said so casually that I wouldn't quickly realize that they were being addressed to me. When I did, I would be paralyzed with embarrassment, unable to return the insult. (Those times I happened to be with white grammar school friends, *they* shouted back. Imbued with the mysterious kindness of children, my friends would never ask later why I hadn't yelled out in my own defense.)

In all, there could not have been more than a dozen incidents of name-calling. That there were so few suggests that I was not a primary victim of racial abuse. But that, even today, I can clearly remember particular incidents is proof of their impact. Because of such incidents, I listened when my parents remarked that Mexicans were often mistreated in California border towns. And in Texas. I listened carefully when I heard that two of my cousins had been refused admittance to an 'all-white' swimming pool. And that an uncle had been told by some man to go back to Africa. I followed the progress of the southern black civil rights movement, which was gaining prominent notice in Sacramento's afternoon newspaper. But what most intrigued me was the connection between dark skin and poverty. Because I heard my mother speak so often about the relegation of dark people to menial labor, I considered the great victims of racism to be those who were poor and forced to do menial work. People like the farmworkers whose skin was dark from the sun.

After meeting a black grammar school friend of my sister's, I remember thinking that she wasn't really 'black.' What interested me was the fact that she wasn't poor. (Her well-dressed parents would come by after work to pick her up in a shiny green Oldsmobile.) By contrast, the garbage men who appeared every Friday morning seemed to me unmistakably black. (I didn't bother to ask my parents why Sacramento garbage men always were black. I thought I knew.) One morning I was in the backyard when a man opened the gate. He was an ugly, square-faced black man with popping red eyes, a pail slung over his shoulder. As he approached, I stood up. And in a voice that seemed to me very weak, I piped, 'Hi.' But the man paid me no heed. He strode past to the can by the garage. In a single broad movement, he overturned its contents into his larger pail. Our can came crashing down as he turned and left me watching, in awe.

'*Pobres negros*,' my mother remarked when she'd notice a headline in the paper about a civil rights demonstration in the South. 'How the *gringos* mistreat them.' In the same tone of voice she'd tell me about the mistreatment her brother endured years before. (After my grandfather's death, my grandmother had come to America with her son and five daughters.) 'My sisters, we were still all just teenagers. And since *mi pápa* was dead, my brother had to be the head of the family. He had to support us, to find work. But what skills did he have! Twenty years old. *Pobre*. He was tall, like your grandfather. And strong. He did construction work. "Construction!" The *gringos* kept him digging all day, doing the dirtiest jobs. And they would pay him next to nothing. Sometimes they promised him one salary and paid him less when he finished. But what could he do? Report them? We weren't citizens then. He didn't even know English. And he was dark. What chances could he have? As soon as we sisters got older, he went right back to Mexico. He hated this country. He looked so tired when he left. Already with a hunchback. Still in his twenties. But old-looking. No life for him here. *Pobre.*'

Dark skin was for my mother the most important symbol of a life of oppressive labor and poverty. But both my parents recognized other symbols as well.

My father noticed the feel of every hand he shook. (He'd smile sometimes – marvel more than scorn – remembering a man he'd met who had soft, uncalloused hands.)

My mother would grab a towel in the kitchen and rub my oily face sore when I came in from playing outside. 'Clean the *grasa* off of your face!' (*Greaser!*)

Symbols: When my older sister, then in high school, asked my mother if she could do light housework in the afternoons for a rich lady we knew, my mother was frightened by the idea. For several weeks she troubled over it before granting conditional permission: 'Just remember, you're not a maid. I don't want you wearing a uniform.' My father echoed the same warning. Walking with him past a hotel, I watched as he stared at a doorman dressed like a Beefeater. 'How can anyone let himself be dressed up like that? Like a clown. Don't you ever get a job where you have to put on a uniform.' In summertime neighbors would ask me if I wanted to earn extra money by mowing their lawns. Again and again my mother worried: 'Why did they ask *you?* Can't you find anything better?' Inevitably, she'd relent. She knew I needed the money. But I was

instructed to work after dinner. ('When the sun's not so hot.')
Even then, I'd have to wear a hat. *Un sombrero de* baseball.

(*Sombrero*. Watching gray cowboy movies, I'd brood over
the meaning of the broad-rimmed hat – that troubling symbol
– which comically distinguished a Mexican cowboy from real
cowboys.)

From my father came no warnings concerning the sun. His
fear was of dark factory jobs. He remembered too well his first
jobs when he came to this country, not intending to stay, just
to earn money enough to sail on to Australia. (In Mexico he
had heard too many stories of discrimination in *los Estados
Unidos*. So it was Australia, that distant island-continent, that
loomed in his imagination as his 'America.') The work my
father found in San Francisco was work for the unskilled. A
factory job. Then a cannery job. (He'd remember the noise
and the heat.) Then a job at a warehouse. (He'd remember the
dark stench of old urine.) At one place there were fistfights;
at another a supervisor who hated Chinese and Mexicans. Nowhere a union.

His memory of himself in those years is held by those jobs.
Never making money enough for passage to Australia; slowly
giving up the plan of returning to school to resume his third-
grade education – to become an engineer. My memory of him
in those years, however, is lifted from photographs in the family album which show him on his honeymoon with my mother
– the woman who had convinced him to stay in America. I have
studied their photographs often, seeking to find in those figures
some clear resemblance to the man and the woman I've known
as my parents. But the youthful faces in the photos remain,
behind dark glasses, shadowy figures anticipating my mother
and father.

They are pictured on the grounds of the Coronado Hotel near San Diego, standing in the pale light of a winter afternoon. She is wearing slacks. Her hair falls seductively over one side of her face. He appears wearing a double-breasted suit, an un-needed raincoat draped over his arm. Another shows them standing together, solemnly staring ahead. Their shoulders barely are touching. There is to their pose an aristocratic for-mality, an elegant Latin hauteur.

The man in those pictures is the same man who was fas-cinated by Italian grand opera. I have never known just what my father saw in the spectacle, but he has told me that he would take my mother to the Opera House every Friday night – if he had money enough for orchestra seats. ('Why go to sit in the balcony?') On Sundays he'd don Italian silk scarves and a camel's hair coat to take his new wife to the polo matches in Golden Gate Park. But one weekend my father stopped going to the opera and polo matches. He would blame the change in his life on one job – a warehouse job, working for a large corpora-tion which today advertises its products with the smiling faces of children. 'They made me an old man before my time,' he'd say to me many years later. Afterward, jobs got easier and cleaner. Eventually, in middle age, he got a job making false teeth. But his youth was spent at the warehouse. 'Everything changed,' his wife remembers. The dapper young man in the old photographs yielded to the man I saw after dinner: hag-gard, asleep on the sofa. During 'The Ed Sullivan Show' on Sunday nights, when Roberta Peters or Licia Albanese would appear on the tiny blue screen, his head would jerk up alert. He'd sit forward while the notes of Puccini sounded before him. ('Un bel dí.')

By the time they had a family, my parents no longer

dressed in very fine clothes. Those symbols of great wealth and the reality of their lives too noisily clashed. No longer did they try to fit themselves, like paper-doll figures, behind trappings so foreign to their actual lives. My father no longer wore silk scarves or expensive wool suits. He sold his tuxedo to a second-hand store for five dollars. My mother sold her rabbit fur coat to the wife of a Spanish radio station disc jockey. ('It looks better on you than it does on me,' she kept telling the lady until the sale was completed.) I was six years old at the time, but I recall watching the transaction with complete understanding. The woman I knew as my mother was already physically un-like the woman in her honeymoon photos. My mother's hair was short. Her shoulders were thick from carrying children. Her fingers were swollen red, toughened by housecleaning. Al-ready my mother would admit to foreseeing herself in her own mother, a woman grown old, bald and bowlegged, after a hard lifetime of working.

In their manner, both my parents continued to respect the symbols of what they considered to be upper-class life. Very early, they taught me the *propio* way of eating *como los ricos*. And I was carefully taught elaborate formulas of polite greet-ing and parting. The dark little boy would be invited by class-mates to the rich houses on Forty-fourth and Forty-fifth streets. 'How do you do?' or 'I am very pleased to meet you,' I would say, bowing slightly to the amused mothers of classmates. 'Thank you very much for the dinner; it was very delicious.'

I made an impression. I intended to make an impression, to be invited back. (I soon realized that the trick was to get the mother or father to notice me.) From those early days began my association with rich people, my fascination with their secret. My mother worried. She warned me not to come home expecting to have the things my friends possessed. But she needn't have said anything. When I went to the big houses, I remembered that I was, at best, a visitor to the world I saw there. For that reason, I was an especially watchful guest. I was my parents' child. Things most middle-class children wouldn't trouble to notice, I studied. Remembered to see: the starched black and white uniform worn by the maid who opened the door; the Mexican gardeners – their complexions as dark as my own. (One gardener's face, glassed by sweat, looked up to see me going inside.)

'Take Richard upstairs and show him your electric train,' the mother said. But it was really the vast polished dining room table I'd come to appraise. Those nights when I was invited to stay for dinner, I'd notice that my friend's mother rang a small silver bell to tell the black woman when to bring in the food. The father, at his end of the table, ate while wearing his tie. When I was not required to speak, I'd skate the icy cut of crystal with my eye; my gaze would follow the golden threads etched onto the rim of china. With my mother's eyes I'd see my hostess's manicured nails and judge them to be marks of her leisure. Later, when my schoolmate's father would bid me goodnight, I would feel his soft fingers and palm when we shook hands. And turning to leave, I'd see my dark self, lit by chandelier light, in a tall hallway mirror.

2

Complexion. My first conscious experience of sexual excitement concerns my complexion. One summer weekend, when I was around seven years old, I was at a public swimming pool with the whole family. I remember sitting on the damp

pavement next to the pool and seeing my mother, in the specta-
tors' bleachers, holding my younger sister on her lap. My
mother, I noticed, was watching my father as he stood on a
diving board, waving to her. I watched her wave back. Then
saw her radiant, bashful, astonishing smile. In that second I
sensed that my mother and father had a relationship I knew
nothing about. A nervous excitement encircled my stomach
as I saw my mother's eyes follow my father's figure curving
into the water. A second or two later, he emerged. I heard him
call out. Smiling, his voice sounded, buoyant, calling me to
swim to him. But turning to see him, I caught my mother's
eye. I heard her shout over to me. In Spanish she called through
the crowd: 'Put a towel on over your shoulders.' In public, she
didn't want to say why. I knew.

That incident anticipates the shame and sexual inferiority
I was to feel in later years because of my dark complexion. I
was to grow up an ugly child. Or one who thought himself
ugly. (*Feo.*) One night when I was eleven or twelve years old,
I locked myself in the bathroom and carefully regarded my
reflection in the mirror over the sink. Without any pleasure I
studied my skin. I turned on the faucet. (In my mind I heard
the swirling voices of aunts, and even my mother's voice, whispering, whispering incessantly about lemon juice solutions and
dark, *feo* children.) With a bar of soap, I fashioned a thick ball
of lather. I began soaping my arms. I took my father's straight
razor out of the medicine cabinet. Slowly, with steady deliber-
ateness, I put the blade against my flesh, pressed it as close as
I could without cutting, and moved it up and down across my
skin to see if I could get out, somehow lessen, the dark. All I
succeeded in doing, however, was in shaving my arms bare of
their hair. For as I noted with disappointment, the dark would

not come out. It remained. Trapped. Deep in the cells of my skin.

Throughout adolescence, I felt myself mysteriously marked. Nothing else about my appearance would concern me so much as the fact that my complexion was dark. My mother would say how sorry she was that there was not money enough to get braces to straighten my teeth. But I never bothered about my teeth. In three-way mirrors at department stores, I'd see my profile dramatically defined by a long nose, but it was really only the color of my skin that caught my attention.

I wasn't afraid that I would become a menial laborer because of my skin. Nor did my complexion make me feel especially vulnerable to racial abuse. (I didn't really consider my dark skin to be a racial characteristic. I would have been only too happy to look as Mexican as my light-skinned older brother.) Simply, I judged myself ugly. And, since the women in my family had been the ones who discussed it in such worried tones, I felt my dark skin made me unattractive to women.

Thirteen years old. Fourteen. In a grammar school art class, when the assignment was to draw a self-portrait, I tried and I tried but could not bring myself to shade in the face on the paper to anything like my actual tone. With disgust then I would come face to face with myself in mirrors. With disappointment I located myself in class photographs – my dark face undefined by the camera which had clearly described the white faces of classmates. Or I'd see my dark wrist against my long-sleeved white shirt.

I grew divorced from my body. Insecure, overweight, listless. On hot summer days when my rubber-soled shoes soaked up the heat from the sidewalk, I kept my head down. Or walked in the shade. My mother didn't need anymore to tell me to watch out for the sun. I denied myself a sensational life. The normal, extraordinary, animal excitement of feeling my body alive – riding shirtless on a bicycle in the warm wind created by furious self-propelled motion – the sensations that first had excited in me a sense of my maleness, I denied. I was too ashamed of my body. I wanted to forget that I had a body because I had a brown body. I was grateful that none of my classmates ever mentioned the fact.

I continued to see the *braceros*, those men I resembled in one way and, in another way, didn't resemble at all. On the watery horizon of a Valley afternoon, I'd see them. And though I feared looking like them, it was with silent envy that I regarded them still. I envied them their physical lives, their freedom to violate the taboo of the sun. Closer to home I would notice the shirtless construction workers, the roofers, the sweating men tarring the street in front of the house. And I'd see the Mexican gardeners. I was unwilling to admit the attraction of their lives. I tried to deny it by looking away. But what was denied became strongly desired.

In high school physical education classes, I withdrew, in the regular company of five or six classmates, to a distant corner of a football field where we smoked and talked. Our company was composed of bodies too short or too tall, all graceless and all – except mine – pale. Our conversation was usually witty. (In fact we were intelligent.) If we referred to the athletic contests around us, it was with sarcasm. With savage scorn I'd refer to the 'animals' playing football or baseball. It would have been important for me to have joined them. Or for me to have taken off my shirt, to have let the sun burn dark on my skin, and to have run barefoot on the warm wet grass. It would have been very important. Too important. It would have been too telling a gesture – to admit the desire for sensation, the body, my body.

Fifteen, sixteen. I was a teenager shy in the presence of girls. Never dated. Barely could talk to a girl without stammering. In high school I went to several dances, but I never managed to ask a girl to dance. So I stopped going. I cannot remember high school years now with the parade of typical images: bright drive-ins or gliding blue shadows of a Junior Prom. At home most weekend nights, I would pass evenings reading. Like those hidden, precocious adolescents who have no real-life sexual experiences, I read a great deal of romantic fiction. 'You won't find it in your books,' my brother would playfully taunt me as he prepared to go to a party by freezing the crest of the wave in his hair with sticky pomade. Through my reading, however, I developed a fabulous and sophisticated sexual imagination. At seventeen, I may not have known how to engage a girl in small talk, but I had read *Lady Chatterley's Lover*.

It annoyed me to hear my father's teasing: that I would never know what 'real work' is; that my hands were so soft. I think I knew it was his way of admitting pleasure and pride in my academic success. But I didn't smile. My mother said she was glad her children were getting their educations and would not be pushed around like *los pobres*. I heard the remark ironically as a reminder of my separation from *los braceros*. At such times I suspected that education was making me effeminate. The odd thing, however, was that I did not judge my classmates so harshly. Nor did I consider my male teachers in high school effeminate. It was only myself I judged against some shadowy, mythical Mexican laborer – dark like me, yet very different.

Language was crucial. I knew that I had violated the ideal of the *macho* by becoming such a dedicated student of language and literature. *Machismo* was a word never exactly defined by the persons who used it. (It was best described in the 'proper' behavior of men.) Women at home, nevertheless, would repeat the old Mexican dictum that a man should be *feo, fuerte, y formal.* 'The three *F*'s,' my mother called them, smiling slyly. *Feo* I took to mean not literally ugly so much as ruggedly handsome. (When my mother and her sisters spent a loud, laughing afternoon determining ideal male good looks, they finally settled on the actor Gilbert Roland, who was neither too pretty nor ugly but had looks 'like a man.') *Fuerte,* 'strong,' seemed to mean not physical strength as much as inner strength, character. A dependable man is *fuerte. Fuerte* for that reason was a characteristic subsumed by the last of the three qualities, and the one I most often considered – *formal.* To be *formal* is to be steady. A man of responsibility, a good provider. Someone *formal* is also constant. A person to be relied upon in adversity. A sober man, a man of high seriousness.

I learned a great deal about being *formal* just by listening to the way my father and other male relatives of his generation spoke. A man was not silent necessarily. Nor was he limited in the tones he could sound. For example, he could tell a long, involved, humorous story and laugh at his own humor with high-pitched giggling. But a man was not talkative the way a woman could be. It was permitted a woman to be gossipy and chatty. (When one heard many voices in a room, it was usually women who were talking.) Men spoke much less rapidly. And often men spoke in monologues. (When one voice sounded in a crowded room, it was most often a man's voice one heard.) More important than any of this was the fact that a man never verbally revealed his emotions. Men did not speak about their unease in moments of crisis or danger. It was the woman who worried aloud when her husband got laid off from work. At times of illness or death in the family, a man was usually quiet, even silent. Women spoke up to voice prayers. In distress, women always sounded quick ejaculations to God or the Virgin; women prayed in clearly audible voices at a wake held in a funeral parlor. And on the subject of love, a woman was verbally expansive. She spoke of her yearning and delight. A married man, if he spoke publicly about love, usually did so with playful, mischievous irony. Younger, unmarried men more often were quiet. (The *macho* is a silent suitor. *Formal.*)

At home I was quiet, so perhaps I seemed *formal* to my relations and other Spanish-speaking visitors to the house. But outside the house – my God! – I talked. Particularly in class or alone with my teachers, I chattered. (Talking seemed to make teachers think I was bright.) I often was proud of my way with words. Though, on other occasions, for example, when I would hear my mother busily speaking to women, it would occur to me that my attachment to words made me like her. Her son. Not *formal* like my father. At such times I even suspected that my nostalgia for sounds – the noisy, intimate Spanish sounds of my past – was nothing more than effeminate yearning.

High school English teachers encouraged me to describe very personal feelings in words. Poems and short stories I wrote, expressing sorrow and loneliness, were awarded high grades. In my bedroom were books by poets and novelists – books that I loved – in which male writers published feelings the men in my family never revealed or acknowledged in words. And it seemed to me that there was something unmanly about my attachment to literature. Even today, when so much about the myth of the *macho* no longer concerns me, I cannot altogether evade such notions. Writing these pages, admitting my embarrassment or my guilt, admitting my sexual anxieties and my physical insecurity, I have not been able to forget that I am not being *formal*.

So be it.

3

I went to college at Stanford, attracted partly by its academic reputation, partly because it was the school rich people went to. I found myself on a campus with golden children of western America's upper middle class. Many were students both ambitious for academic success *and* accustomed to leisured life in the sun. In the afternoon, they lay spread out, sunbathing in front of the library, reading Swift or Engels or Beckett. Others went by in convertibles, off to play tennis or ride horses or sail. Beach boys dressed in tank-tops and shorts were my classmates in undergraduate seminars. Tall tan girls wearing white strapless dresses sat directly in front of me in lecture rooms. I'd study them, their physical confidence. I was still recognizably kin to the boy I had been. Less tortured perhaps. But still kin. At Stanford, it's true, I began to have something like a conventional sexual life. I don't think, however, that I really believed that the women I knew found me physically appealing. I continued to stay out of the sun. I didn't linger in mirrors. And I was the student at Stanford who remembered to notice the Mexican-American janitors and gardeners working on campus.

It was at Stanford, one day near the end of my senior year, that a friend told me about a summer construction job he knew was available. I was quickly alert. Desire uncoiled within me. My friend said that he knew I had been looking for summer employment. He knew I needed some money. Almost apologetically he explained: It was something I probably wouldn't be interested in, but a friend of his, a contractor, needed someone for the summer to do menial jobs. There would be lots of shoveling and raking and sweeping. Nothing too hard. But nothing more interesting either. Still, the pay would be good. Did I want it? Or did I know someone who did?

I did. Yes, I said, surprised to hear myself say it.

In the weeks following, friends cautioned that I had no idea how hard physical labor really is. ('You only *think* you know what it is like to shovel for eight hours straight.') Their objections seemed to me challenges. They resolved the issue. I became happy with my plan. I decided, however, not to tell my parents. I wouldn't tell my mother because I could guess her worried reaction. I would tell my father only after the summer was over, when I could announce that, after all, I did know what 'real work' is like.

The day I met the contractor (a Princeton graduate, it turned out), he asked me whether I had done any physical labor before. 'In high school, during the summer,' I lied. And although he seemed to regard me with skepticism, he decided to give me a try. Several days later, expectant, I arrived at my first construction site. I would take off my shirt to the sun. And at last grasp desired sensation. No longer afraid. At last become like a *bracero*. 'We need those tree stumps out of here by tomorrow,' the contractor said. I started to work.

I labored with excitement that first morning – and all the days after. The work was harder than I could have expected. But it was never as tedious as my friends had warned me it would be. There was too much physical pleasure in the labor. Especially early in the day, I would be most alert to the sensations of movement and straining. Beginning around seven each morning (when the air was still damp but the scent of weeds and dry earth anticipated the heat of the sun), I would feel my body resist the first thrusts of the shovel. My arms, tightened by sleep, would gradually loosen; after only several minutes, sweat would gather in beads on my forehead and then – a short while later – I would feel my chest silky with sweat in the breeze. I would return to my work. A nervous spark of pain would fly up my arm and settle to burn like an ember in the thick of my shoulder. An hour, two passed. Three. My whole body would assume regular movements; my shoveling would be described by identical, even movements. Even later in the day, my enthusiasm for primitive sensation would survive the heat and the dust and the insects pricking my back. I would strain wildly for sensation as the day came to a close. At three-thirty, quitting time, I would stand upright and slowly let my head fall back, luxuriating in the feeling of tightness relieved.

Some of the men working nearby would watch me and laugh. Two or three of the older men took the trouble to teach me the right way to use a pick, the correct way to shovel. 'You're doing it wrong, too fucking hard,' one man scolded. Then proceeded to show me – what persons who work with their bodies all their lives quickly learn – the most economical way to use one's body in labor.

'Don't make your back do so much work,' he instructed. I stood impatiently listening, half listening, vaguely watching, then noticed his work-thickened fingers clutching the shovel. I was annoyed. I wanted to tell him that I enjoyed shoveling the wrong way. And I didn't want to learn the right way. I wasn't afraid of back pain. I liked the way my body felt sore at the end of the day.

I was about to, but, as it turned out, I didn't say a thing. Rather it was at that moment I realized that I was fooling myself if I expected a few weeks of labor to gain me admission to the world of the laborer. I would not learn in three months what my father had meant by 'real work.' I was not bound to this job; I could imagine its rapid conclusion. For me the sensations of exertion and fatigue could be savored. For my father or uncle, working at comparable jobs when they were my age, such sensations were to be feared. Fatigue took a different toll on their bodies – and minds.

It was, I know, a simple insight. But it was with this realization that I took my first step that summer toward realizing something even more important about the 'worker.' In the company of carpenters, electricians, plumbers, and painters at lunch, I would often sit quietly, observant. I was not shy in such company. I felt easy, pleased by the knowledge that I was casually accepted, my presence taken for granted by men (exotics) who worked with their hands. Some days the younger men would talk and talk about sex, and they would howl at women who drove by in cars. Other days the talk at lunchtime was subdued; men gathered in separate groups. It depended on who was around. There were rough, good-natured workers. Others were quiet. The more I remember that summer, the more I realize that there was no single *type* of worker. I am embarrassed to say I had not expected such diversity. I certainly had not expected to meet, for example, a plumber who was an abstract painter in his off hours and admired the work of Mark Rothko. Nor did I expect to meet so many workers with college diplomas. (They were the ones who were not surprised that I intended to enter graduate school in the fall.) I suppose what I really want to say here is painfully obvious, but I must say it nevertheless: The men of that summer were middle-class Americans. They certainly didn't constitute an oppressed society. Carefully completing their work sheets; talking about the fortunes of local football teams; planning Las Vegas vacations; comparing the gas mileage of various makes of campers – they were not *los pobres* my mother had spoken about.

On two occasions, the contractor hired a group of Mexican aliens. They were employed to cut down some trees and haul off debris. In all, there were six men of varying age. The youngest in his late twenties; the oldest (his father?) perhaps sixty years old. They came and they left in a single old truck. Anonymous men. They were never introduced to the other men at the site. Immediately upon their arrival, they would follow the contractor's directions, start working – rarely resting – seemingly driven by a fatalistic sense that work which had to be done was best done as quickly as possible.

I watched them sometimes. Perhaps they watched me. The only time I saw them pay me much notice was one day at lunchtime when I was laughing with the other men. The Mexicans sat apart when they ate, just as they worked by themselves. Quiet. I rarely heard them say much to each other. All I could hear were their voices calling out sharply to one another, giving directions. Otherwise, when they stood briefly resting, they talked among themselves in voices too hard to overhear.

The contractor knew enough Spanish, and the Mexicans – or at least the oldest of them, their spokesman – seemed to know enough English to communicate. But because I was around, the contractor decided one day to make me his translator. (He assumed I could speak Spanish.) I did what I was told. Shyly I went over to tell the Mexicans that the *patrón* wanted them to do something else before they left for the day. As I started to speak, I was afraid with my old fear that I would be unable to pronounce the Spanish words. But it was a simple instruction I had to convey. I could say it in phrases.

The dark sweating faces turned toward me as I spoke. They stopped their work to hear me. Each nodded in response. I stood there. I wanted to say something more. But what could I say in Spanish, even if I could have pronounced the words right? Perhaps I just wanted to engage them in small talk, to be assured of their confidence, our familiarity. I thought for a moment to ask them where in Mexico they were from. Something like that. And maybe I wanted to tell them (a lie, if need be) that my parents were from the same part of Mexico.

I stood there.

Their faces watched me. The eyes of the man directly in front of me moved slowly over my shoulder, and I turned to follow his glance toward *el patrón* some distance away. For a moment I felt swept up by that glance into the Mexicans' company. But then I heard one of them returning to work. And then the others went back to work. I left them without saying anything more.

When they had finished, the contractor went over to pay them in cash. (He later told me that he paid them collectively – 'for the job,' though he wouldn't tell me their wages. He said something quickly about the good rate of exchange 'in their own country.') I can still hear the loudly confident voice he used with the Mexicans. It was the sound of the *gringo* I had heard as a very young boy. And I can still hear the quiet, indistinct sounds of the Mexican, the oldest, who replied. At hearing that voice I was sad for the Mexicans. Depressed by their vulnerability. Angry at myself. The adventure of the summer seemed suddenly ludicrous. I would not shorten the distance I felt from *los pobres* with a few weeks of physical labor. I would not become like them. They were different from me.

After that summer, a great deal – and not very much really – changed in my life. The curse of physical shame was broken by the sun; I was no longer ashamed of my body. No longer would I deny myself the pleasing sensations of my maleness. During those years when middle-class black Americans began to assert with pride, 'Black is beautiful,' I was able to regard my complexion without shame. I am today darker than I ever was as a boy. I have taken up the middle-class sport of long-distance running. Nearly every day now I run ten or fifteen miles, barely clothed, my skin exposed to the California winter rain and wind or the summer sun of late afternoon. The torso, the soccer player's calves and thighs, the arms of the twenty-year-old I never was, I possess now in my thirties. I study the youthful parody shape in the mirror: the stomach lipped tight by muscle; the shoulders rounded by chin-ups; the arms veined strong. This man. A man. I meet him. He laughs to see me, what I have become.

The dandy. I wear double-breasted Italian suits and custom-made English shoes. I resemble no one so much as my father – the man pictured in those honeymoon photos. At that point in life when he abandoned the dandy's posture, I assume it. At the point when my parents would not consider going on vacation, I register at the Hotel Carlyle in New York and the Plaza Athenée in Paris. I am as taken by the symbols of leisure and wealth as they were. For my parents, however, those symbols became taunts, reminders of all they could not achieve in

one lifetime. For me those same symbols are reassuring reminders of public success. I tempt vulgarity to be reassured. I am
filled with the gaudy delight, the monstrous grace of the
nouveau riche.

In recent years I have had occasion to lecture in ghetto high
schools. There I see students of remarkable style and physical
grace. (One can see more dandies in such schools than one ever
will find in middle-class high schools.) There is not the look of
casual assurance I saw students at Stanford display. Ghetto girls
mimic high-fashion models. Their dresses are of bold, forceful
color; their figures elegant, long; the stance theatrical. Boys
wear shirts that grip at their overdeveloped muscular bodies.
(Against a powerless future, they engage images of strength.)
Bad nutrition does not yet tell. Great disappointment, fatal to
youth, awaits them still. For the moment, movements in school
hallways are dancelike, a procession of postures in a sexual
masque. Watching them, I feel a kind of envy. I wonder how
different my adolescence would have been had I been free. . . .
But no, it is my parents I see – their optimism during those years
when they were entertained by Italian grand opera.

The registration clerk in London wonders if I have just
been to Switzerland. And the man who carries my luggage in
New York guesses the Caribbean. My complexion becomes a
mark of my leisure. Yet no one would regard my complexion
the same way if I entered such hotels through the service entrance. That is only to say that my complexion assumes its
significance from the context of my life. My skin, in itself,
means nothing. I stress the point because I know there are
people who would label me 'disadvantaged' because of my
color. They make the same mistake I made as a boy, when I

thought a disadvantaged life was circumscribed by particular occupations. That summer I worked in the sun may have made me physically indistinguishable from the Mexicans working nearby. (My skin was actually darker because, unlike them, I worked without wearing a shirt. By late August my hands were probably as tough as theirs.) But I was not one of *los pobres*. What made me different from them was an attitude of *mind*, my imagination of myself.

I do not blame my mother for warning me away from the sun when I was young. In a world where her brother had become an old man in his twenties because he was dark, my complexion was something to worry about. 'Don't run in the sun,' she warns me today. I run. In the end, my father was right – though perhaps he did not know how right or why – to say that I would never know what real work is. I will never know what he felt at his last factory job. If tomorrow I worked at some kind of factory, it would go differently for me. My long education would favor me. I could act as a public person – able to defend my interests, to unionize, to petition, to speak up – to challenge and demand. (I will never know what real work is.) I will never know what the Mexicans knew, gathering their shovels and ladders and saws.

Their silence stays with me now. The wages those Mexicans received for their labor were only a measure of their disadvantaged condition. Their silence is more telling. They lack a public identity. They remain profoundly alien. Persons apart. People lacking a union obviously, people without grounds. They depend upon the relative good will or fairness of their employers each day. For such people, lacking a better alternative, it is not such an unreasonable risk.

Their silence stays with me. I have taken these many words to describe its impact. Only: the quiet. Something uncanny about it. Its compliance. Vulnerability. Pathos. As I heard their truck rumbling away, I shuddered, my face mirrored with sweat. I had finally come face to face with *los pobres.*

FIVE

Profession

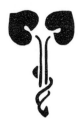

Minority student – that was the label I bore in college at Stanford, then in graduate school at Columbia and Berkeley: a nonwhite reader of Spenser and Milton and Austen.

In the late 1960s nonwhite Americans clamored for access to higher education, and I became a principal beneficiary of the academy's response, its programs of affirmative action. My presence was noted each fall by the campus press office in its proud tally of Hispanic-American students enrolled; my progress was followed by HEW statisticians. One of the lucky ones. Rewarded. Advanced for belonging to a racial group 'underrepresented' in American institutional life. When I sought admission to graduate schools, when I applied for fellowships and summer study grants, when I needed a teaching assistantship, my Spanish surname or the dark mark in the space indicating my race – 'check one' – nearly always got me whatever I asked for. When the time came for me to look for a college teaching job (the end of my years as a scholarship boy), potential employers came looking for me – a minority student.

Fittingly, it falls to me, as someone who so awkwardly carried the label, to question it now, its juxtaposition of terms – minority, student. For me there is no way to say it with grace. I say it rather with irony sharpened by self-pity. I say it with anger. It is a term that should never have been foisted on me. One I was wrong to accept.

In college one day a professor of English returned my term paper with this comment penciled just under the grade: 'Maybe the reason you feel Dickens's sense of alienation so acutely is because you are a minority student.' *Minority student.* It was the first time I had seen the expression; I remember sensing that it somehow referred to my race. Never before had a teacher suggested that my academic performance was linked to my racial identity. After class I reread the remark several times. Around me other students were talking and leaving. The professor remained in front of the room, collecting his papers and books. I was about to go up and question his note. But I didn't. I let the comment pass; thus became implicated in the strange reform movement that followed.

The year was 1967. And what I did not realize was that my life would be radically changed by deceptively distant events. In 1967, their campaign against southern segregation laws successful at last, black civil rights leaders were turning their attention to the North, a North they no longer saw in contrast to the South. What they realized was that although no official restrictions denied blacks access to northern institutions of advancement and power, for most blacks this freedom was only theoretical. (The obstacle was 'institutional racism.') Activists made their case against institutions of higher education. Schools like Wisconsin and Princeton long had been open to blacks. But the tiny number of nonwhite students and faculty members at such schools suggested that there was more than the issue of access to consider. Most blacks simply couldn't afford tuition for higher education. And, because the primary and secondary schooling blacks received was usually poor, few qualified for admission. Many were so culturally alienated that they never thought to apply; they couldn't even imagine themselves going to college.

I think – as I thought in 1967 – that the black civil rights leaders were correct: Higher education was not, nor is it yet, accessible to many black Americans. I think now, however, that the activists tragically limited the impact of their movement with the reforms they proposed. Seeing the problem solely in racial terms (as a case of *de facto* segregation), they pressured universities and colleges to admit more black students and hire more black faculty members. There were demands for financial aid programs. And tutoring help. And more aggressive student recruitment. But this was all. The aim was to integrate higher education in the North. So no one seemed troubled by the fact that those who were in the best position to benefit from such reforms were those blacks least victimized by racism or any other social oppression – those culturally, if not always economically, of the middle class.

The lead established, other civil rights groups followed. Soon Hispanic-American activists began to complain that there were too few Hispanics in colleges. They concluded that this was the result of racism. They offered racial solutions. They demanded that Hispanic-American professors be hired. And that students with Spanish surnames be admitted in greater numbers to colleges. Shortly after, I was 'recognized' on campus: an Hispanic-American, a 'Latino,' a Mexican-American, a 'Chicano.' No longer would people ask me, as I had been asked before, if I were a foreign student. (From India? Peru?) All of a sudden everyone seemed to know – as the professor of English had known – that I was a minority student.

I became a highly rewarded minority student. For campus officials came first to students like me with their numerous offers of aid. And why not? Administrators met their angriest critics' demands by promoting any plausible Hispanic on hand. They were able, moreover, to use the presence of conventionally qualified nonwhite students like me to prove that they were meeting the goals of their critics.

In 1969, the assassination of Dr. Martin Luther King, Jr., prompted many academic officials to commit themselves publicly to the goal of integrating their institutions. One day I watched the nationally televised funeral; a week later I received invitations to teach at community colleges. There were opportunities to travel to foreign countries with contingents of 'minority group scholars.' And I went to the financial aid office on campus and was handed special forms for minority student applicants. I was a minority student, wasn't I? the lady behind the counter asked me rhetorically. Yes, I said. Carelessly said. I completed the application. Was later awarded.

In a way, it was true. I was a minority. The word, as popularly used, did describe me. In the sixties, *minority* became a synonym for socially disadvantaged Americans – but it was primarily a numerical designation. The word referred to entire races and nationalities of Americans, those numerically underrepresented in institutional life. (Thus, without contradiction, one could speak of 'minority groups.') And who were they exactly? Blacks – all blacks – most obviously were minorities. And Hispanic-Americans. And American Indians. And some others. (It was left to federal statisticians, using elaborate surveys and charts, to determine which others precisely.)

I was a minority.

I believed it. For the first several years, I accepted the label. I certainly supported the racial civil rights movement; supported the goal of broadening access to higher education. But there was a problem: One day I listened approvingly to a government official defend affirmative action; the next day *I* realized the benefits of the program. I was the minority student the political activists shouted about at noontime rallies. Against their rhetoric, I stood out in relief, unrelieved. *Knowing*: I was not really more socially disadvantaged than the white graduate students in my classes. *Knowing*: I was not disadvantaged like many of the new nonwhite students who were entering college, lacking good early schooling.

Nineteen sixty-nine. 1970. 1971. Slowly, slowly, the term *minority* became a source of unease. It would remind me of those boyhood years when I had felt myself alienated from public (majority) society – *los gringos. Minority. Minorities. Minority groups.* The terms sounded in public to remind me in private of the truth: I was not – in a *cultural* sense – a minority, an alien from public life. (Not like *los pobres* I had encountered during my recent laboring summer.) The truth was summarized in the sense of irony I'd feel at hearing myself called a minority student: The reason I was no longer a minority was because I had become a student.

Minority student!

In conversations with faculty members I began to worry the issue, only to be told that my unease was unfounded. A dean said he was certain that after I graduated I would be able to work among 'my people.' A senior faculty member expressed his confidence that, though I was unrepresentative of lower-class Hispanics, I would serve as a role model for others of my race. Another faculty member was sure that I would be a valued counselor to incoming minority students. (He assumed that, because of my race, I retained a special capacity for communicating with nonwhite students.) I also heard academic officials say that minority students would someday form a leadership class in America. (From our probable positions of power, we would be able to lobby for reforms to benefit others of our race.)

In 1973 I wrote and had published two essays in which I said that I had been educated away from the culture of my

mother and father. In 1974 I published an essay admitting unease over becoming the beneficiary of affirmative action. There
was another article against affirmative action in 1977. One more
soon after. At times, I proposed contrary ideas; consistent always
was the admission that I was no longer like socially disadvantaged Hispanic-Americans. But this admission, made in national magazines, only brought me a greater degree of success.
A published minority student, I won a kind of celebrity. In my
mail were admiring letters from right-wing politicians. There
were also invitations to address conferences of college administrators or government officials.

My essays served as my 'authority' to speak at the Marriott
Something or the Sheraton Somewhere. To stand at a ballroom
podium and hear my surprised echo sound from a microphone.
I spoke. I started getting angry letters from activists. One wrote
to say that I was becoming the *gringos'* fawning pet. What
'they' want all Hispanics to be. I remembered the remark when
I was introduced to an all-white audience and heard their ap-
plause so loud. I remembered the remark when I stood in a university auditorium and saw an audience of brown and black faces
watching me. I publicly wondered whether a person like me
should really be termed a minority. But some members of the
audience thought I was denying racial pride, trying somehow
to deny my racial identity. They rose to protest. One Mexican-
American said I was a minority whether I wanted to be or not.
And he said that the reason I was a beneficiary of affirmative
action was simple: I was a Chicano. (Wasn't I?) It was only an
issue of race.

It is important now to remember that the early leaders of the
northern civil rights movement were from the South. (The civil
rights movement in the North depended upon an understand-

ing of racism derived from the South.) Here was the source of the mistaken strategy – the reason why activists could so easily ignore class and could consider race alone a sufficient measure of social oppression. In the South, where racism had been legally enforced, all blacks suffered discrimination uniformly. The black businessman and the black maid were undifferentiated by the law that forced them to the rear of the bus. Thus, when segregation laws were challenged and finally defeated, the benefit to one became a benefit for all; the integration of an institution by a single black implied an advance for the entire race.

From the experience of southern blacks, a generation of Americans came to realize with new force that there are forms of oppression that touch all levels of a society. This was the crucial lesson that survived the turbulence in the South of the fifties and sixties. The southern movement gave impetus initially to the civil rights drives of nonwhite Americans in the North. Later, the black movement's vitality extended to animate the liberation movements of women, the elderly, the physically disabled, and the homosexual. Leaders of these groups described the oppression they suffered by analogy to that suffered by blacks. Thus one heard of sexism – that echo of racism, and something called gray power. People in wheelchairs gave the black-power salute. And homosexuals termed themselves 'America's last niggers.' As racism rhetorically replaced poverty as the key social oppression, Americans learned to look beyond class in considering social oppression. The public conscience was enlarged. Americans were able to take seriously, say, the woman business executive's claim to be the victim of social oppression. But with this advance there was a danger. It became easy to underestimate, even to ignore altogether, the importance of *class*. Easy to forget that those whose lives are shaped by poverty and poor education (cultural minorities) are least able to defend themselves against social oppression, whatever its form.

In the era of affirmative action it became more and more difficult to distinguish the middle-class victim of social oppression from the lower-class victim. In fact, it became hard to say when a person ever *stops* being disadvantaged. Quite apart from poverty, the variety of social oppressions that most concerned Americans involved unchangeable conditions. (One does not ever stop being a woman; one does not stop being aged – short of death; one does not stop being a quadriplegic.) The commonplace heard in the sixties was precisely this: A black never stops being black. (The assertion became a kind of justification for affirmative action.)

For my part I believe the black lawyer who tells me that there is never a day in his life when he forgets he is black. I believe the black business executive who says that, although he drives an expensive foreign car, he must be especially wary when a policeman stops him for speeding. I do not doubt that middle-class blacks need to remain watchful when they look for jobs or try to rent or when they travel to unfamiliar towns. 'You can't know what it is like for us,' a black woman shouted at me one day from an audience somewhere. Like a white liberal, I was awed, shaken by her rage; I gave her the point. But now I must insist, must risk presumption to say that I do not think that all blacks are equally 'black.' Surely those uneducated and poor will remain most vulnerable to racism. It was not coincidence that the leadership of the southern civil rights movement was drawn mainly from a well-educated black middle class. Even in the South of the 1950s, all blacks were not equally black.

All Mexican-Americans certainly are not equally Mexican-American. The policy of affirmative action, however, was never able to distinguish someone like me (a graduate student of English, ambitious for a college teaching career) from a slightly educated Mexican-American who lived in a barrio and worked as a menial laborer, never expecting a future improved. Worse, affirmative action made me the beneficiary of his condition. Such was the foolish logic of this program of social reform: Because many Hispanics were absent from higher education, I became with my matriculation an exception, a numerical minority. Because I was not a cultural minority, I was extremely well placed to enjoy the advantages of affirmative action. I was groomed for a position in the multiversity's leadership class.

Remarkably, affirmative action passed as a program of the Left. In fact, its supporters ignored the most fundamental assumptions of the classical Left by disregarding the importance of class and by assuming that the disadvantages of the lower class would necessarily be ameliorated by the creation of an elite society. The movement that began so nobly in the South, in the North came to parody social reform. Those least disadvantaged were helped first, advanced because many others of their race were more disadvantaged. The strategy of affirmative action, finally, did not take seriously the educational dilemma of disadvantaged students. They need good early schooling! Activists pushed to get more nonwhite students into colleges. Meritocratic standards were dismissed as exclusionary. But activists should have asked why so many minority students could not meet those standards; why so many more would never be in a position to apply. The revolutionary demand would have called for a reform of primary and secondary schools.

To improve the education of disadvantaged students requires social changes which educational institutions alone cannot make, of course. Parents of such students need jobs and good housing; the students themselves need to grow up with three meals a day, in safe neighborhoods. But disadvantaged students also require good teachers. Good teachers – not fancy electronic gadgets – to teach them to read and to write. Teachers who are not overwhelmed; teachers with sufficient time to devote to individual students; to inspire. In the late sixties, civil rights activists might have harnessed the great idealism that the southern movement inspired in Americans. They might have called on teachers, might have demanded some kind of national literacy campaign for children of the poor – white and nonwhite – at the earliest levels of learning.

But the opportunity passed. The guardians of institutional America in Washington were able to ignore the need for fundamental social changes. College and university administrators could proudly claim that their institutions had yielded, were open to minority groups. (There was proof in a handful of numbers computed each fall.) So less thought had to be given to the procession of teenagers who leave ghetto high schools disadvantaged, badly taught, unable to find decent jobs.

I wish as I write these things that I could be angry at those who mislabeled me. I wish I could enjoy the luxury of self-pity and cast myself as a kind of 'invisible man.' But guilt is not disposed of so easily. The fact is that I complied with affirmative action. I permitted myself to be prized. Even after publicly voicing objections to affirmative action, I accepted its benefits. I continued to indicate my race on applications for financial aid. (It didn't occur to me to leave the question unanswered.) I'd apply for prestigious national fellowships and tell friends that the reason I won was because I was a minority. (This by way of accepting the fellowship money.) I published essays admitting that I was not a minority – saw my by-line in magazines and journals which once had seemed very remote from my life. It was a scholarship boy's dream come true. I enjoyed being – not being – a minority student, the featured speaker. I was invited to lecture at schools that only a few years before would have rejected my application for graduate study. My life was unlike that of any other graduate student I knew. On weekends I flew cross country to say – through a microphone – that I was not a minority.

Someone told me this: A senior faculty member in the English department at Berkeley smirked when my name came up in a conversation. Someone at the sherry party had wondered if the professor had seen my latest article on affirmative action. The professor replied with arch politeness, 'And what does Mr. Rodriguez have to complain about?'

You who read this act of contrition should know that by writing it I seek a kind of forgiveness – not yours. The forgiveness, rather, of those many persons whose absence from higher education permitted me to be classed a minority student. I wish that they would read this. I doubt they ever will.

2

When civil rights leaders first demanded the admission of minority students to higher education, academic officials could have challenged their critics to seek the more important reform of primary and secondary education. Academics might have agreed to commit themselves to the goal of helping more nonwhite students enter college. But they should have simply acknowledged (the truth) that higher education is out of the reach of minorities – poorly schooled, disadvantaged Americans.

That admission would have taken great courage to make. But more than courage was lacking. When educators promised to open their schools, it was partly because they couldn't imagine another response; their schools were rooted in the belief that higher education should be available to all. (This democratic ideal had made possible the post–World War II expansion of higher education.) Academics would have violated their generation's ideal of openness if they had said that their schools couldn't accommodate disadvantaged Americans. To have acknowledged the truth about their schools, moreover, academics would have had to acknowledge their own position of privilege. And that would have been difficult. The middle-class academy does not deeply impress on students or teachers a sense of social advantage. The campus has become a place for 'making it' rather than a place for those who, relatively speaking, 'have it made.' Even academics on the Left who criticized the 'elitism' of higher education seemed not to recognize how different they themselves were from the socially disadvantaged. Many supported affirmative action, assuming that only access kept minority Americans out of college.

So it happened: Academia accepted its so-called minority students. And after the pool of 'desirable' minority students was depleted, more 'provisional' students were admitted. But the academy was prepared to do little more for such students. (Getting admitted to college was for many nonwhite students the easiest obstacle to overcome.) The conspiracy of kindness became a conspiracy of uncaring. Cruelly, callously, admissions committees agreed to overlook serious academic deficiency. I knew students in college then barely able to read, students unable to grasp the function of a sentence. I knew nonwhite graduate students who were bewildered by the requirement to compose a term paper and who each day were humiliated when they couldn't compete with other students in seminars. There were contrived tutoring programs. But many years of inferior schooling could not be corrected with a crowded hour or two of instruction each week. Not surprisingly, among those students with very poor academic preparation, few completed their courses of study. Many dropped out, most blaming themselves for their failure. One fall, six nonwhite students I knew suffered severe mental collapse. None of the professors who had welcomed them to graduate school were around when it came time to take them to the infirmary or to the airport. And the university officials who so diligently took note of those students in their self-serving totals of entering minority students finally took no note of them when they left.

On every campus, on every faculty, there were exceptions – remarkable professors who took it upon themselves to act as tutors, advisors, friends. Rare women and men, always well known to nonwhite students needing help. More common, however, were those faculty members who simply passed their provisional students. Teachers confronted with evidence of a student's inadequate comprehension found it easiest to dispense a grade that moved a student toward meaningless graduation. The new minority students had been treated with such generosity before. That is how many of them had passed through twelve years of grammar and high school, in the end still needing to be considered culturally disadvantaged.

My experience was different. No professor simply passed me. None treated me with condescension. I was well schooled. Ironically, it was because of what I was so well taught in the classroom that my unease over affirmative action deepened. I was instructed to hear in the Renaissance poet's celebration of pastoral life the reminder of his reader's own civic responsibility and power. I learned how a popular novelist like Dickens, writing for a middle-class audience, makes his readers aware of their ability to effect social reform. Teachers made me aware of D. H. Lawrence's felt separation from his working-class father. And I was made to listen to George Orwell's admission that, as a literate man, he would never be able to imagine what it is like to be one of the uneducated poor.

The odd thing was that in the classroom teachers reminded me of both my public identity and power as a student of literature. But outside of class few were willing to recognize that I was, at best, paradoxically named a minority student. Professors I'd approach would usually defend affirmative action. (Perhaps they felt they had to. Perhaps they intended to help me, to relieve my disquiet.) I was told not to worry so much. 'It's possible to be too conscientious about these matters.' One of my best teachers in graduate school seemed surprised that I always brought up the subject. I was not like 'the others,' he confided, as a kind of compliment. Why then did all this minority business concern me so incessantly? Why spend so much valuable time writing and arguing about affirmative action? he wondered. And I saw deluxe editions of Spenser and Dryden ranged on a bookshelf behind him. Now then, he smiled, when was I going to give him that paper comparing Marx and Wordsworth that sounded so promising?

3

Officially the academy never lost its enthusiasm for affirmative action during the years I was a student. But in the early 1970s I remember hearing professors quietly admit their alarm over various aspects of what was then called the Third World Student Movement.

Faculty members were understandably troubled, though most seemed unwilling to make their concern public. As more and more nonwhite students arrived on campus, less well prepared, many of them chose to believe that they were, in some cultural sense, minorities. They imagined themselves belonging to two very different societies. What campus officials had implied about them – through the policy of affirmative action – the students came to believe, seizing upon the idea of belonging at once to academia and to the society of the disadvantaged. Modern-day scholar-workers, indulging in clownish display, adopted ghetto accents and assumed costumes of the rural poor. The students insisted they still were tied to the culture of their past. Nothing in their lives had changed with their matriculation. They would be able to 'go home again.' They were certain, as well, that their enrollment implied a general social advance for many others of their race off campus. (The scholar remained united with his people.)

For some students perhaps these ideas provided a way of accepting benefits suddenly theirs, accruing simply to race. For others these ideas may have served as a way of accommodating themselves to the life of a campus so culturally foreign. Especially in the early years of the Movement, one often heard nonwhite students complain of feeling lost on the campus. There were demands for separate dormitory facilities, clubhouses, separate cafeteria tables, even for soul-food menus. And in the classroom: 'We can't relate to any of this.'

Nonwhite activists began to complain that college and university courses took little account of the lives of nonwhite Americans. Their complaint was well founded. And it implied a startling critique of the academy's tendency toward parochialism. Ultimately, it led to the establishment of ethnic studies departments where courses were offered in such fields as nine-teenth-century black history and Hispanic-American folk art. The activists made a peculiar claim for these classes. They insisted that the courses would alleviate the cultural anxiety of nonwhite students by permitting them to stay in touch with their home culture.

The perspective gained in the classroom or the library does indeed permit an academic to draw nearer to and understand better the culture of the alien poor. But the academic is brought closer to lower-class culture because of his very distance from it. Leisured, and skilled at abstracting from immediate experience, the scholar is able to see how aspects of individual experience constitute a culture. By contrast, the poor have neither the inclination nor the skill to imagine their lives so abstractly. They remain strangers to the way of life the academic constructs so well on paper.

Ethnic studies departments were founded on romantic hopes. And with the new departments were often instituted 'community action' programs. Students were given course credit for work done in working-class neighborhoods. Too often, however, activists encouraged students to believe that they were in league with the poor when, in actuality, any academic who works with the socially disadvantaged is able to be of benefit to them only because he is culturally different from them.

When, for example, Mexican-American students began to proclaim themselves Chicanos, they taught many persons in the barrios of southwestern America to imagine themselves in a new context. *Chicano*, the Spanish word, was a term lower-class Mexican-Americans had long used to name themselves. It was a private word, slangish, even affectionately vulgar, and, when spoken by a stranger, insulting, because it glibly assumed familiarity. Many Mexican-Americans were consequently shocked when they heard the student activist proclaim himself and his listeners Chicanos. What initially they did not understand was that the English word – which meant literally the same thing (Mexican-American) – was a public word, animated by pride and political purpose. '¡*Somos* Chicanos!' the student activist proclaimed, his voice enlarged through a microphone. He thereby taught his listeners to imagine their union with many others like themselves. But the student easily coined the new word because of his very distance from *Chicano* culture.

Let the reader beware at this point: I am not the best person to evaluate the Third World Student Movement. My relationship to many of the self-proclaimed Chicano students was not an easy one. I felt threatened by them. I was made nervous by their insistence that they still were allied to their parents' culture. Walking on campus one day with my mother and father, I relished the surprised look on their faces when they saw some Hispanic students wearing serapes pass by. I needed to laugh at the clownish display. I needed to tell myself that the new minority students were foolish to think themselves unchanged by their schooling. (I needed to justify my own change.)

I never worked in the barrio. I gave myself all the reasons people ever give to explain why they do not work among the disadvantaged. I envied those minority students who graduated to work among lower-class Hispanics at barrio clinics or legal aid centers. I envied them their fluent Spanish. (I had taken Spanish in high school with *gringos*.) But it annoyed me to hear students on campus loudly talking in Spanish or thickening their surnames with rich baroque accents because I distrusted the implied assertion that their tongue proved their bond to the past, to the poor. I spoke in English. I was invited to Chicano student meetings and social events sponsored by *La Raza*. But I never went. I kept my distance. I was a scholarship boy who belonged to an earlier time. I had come to the campus singly; they had come in a group. (It was in the plural that they often referred to themselves – as minority students.) I had been submissive, willing to mimic my teachers, willing to re-form myself in order to become 'educated.' They were proud, claiming that they didn't need to change by becoming students. I had long before accepted the fact that education exacted a great price for its equally great benefits. They denied that price – any loss.

I was glad to get away from those students when I was awarded a Fulbright Fellowship to study in London. I found myself in the British Museum, at first content, reading English Renaissance literature. But then came the crisis: the domed silence; the dusty pages of books all around me; the days accumulating in lists of obsequious footnotes; the wandering doubts about the value of scholarship. My year in Britain came to an end and I rushed to 'come home.' Then quickly discovered that I could not. Could not cast off the culture I had assumed. Living with my parents for the summer, I remained an academic – a kind of anthropologist in the family kitchen, searching for evidence of our 'cultural ties' as we ate dinner together.

In late summer, I decided to finish my dissertation and to accept a one-year teaching assignment at Berkeley. (It was, after all, where I belonged.)

What I learned from my year at the British Museum and from my summer at home, other academics have learned; others have known the impossibility of going home, going back. Going back to Berkeley, however, I returned to a campus where I was still officially designated a minority – still considered by university officials to be in touch with my native culture. And there were minority students to face.

In my department that year there were five black graduate students. We were the only nonwhite students in a department of nearly three hundred. Initially, I was shy of the black students – afraid of what they'd discover about me. But in seminars they would come and sit by me. They trusted the alliance of color. In soft voices – not wanting to be overheard by the white students around us – they spoke to me. And I felt rewarded by their confidences.

But then one afternoon a group of eight or ten Hispanic students came to my office. They wanted me to teach a 'minority literature' course at some barrio community center on Saturday mornings. They were certain that this new literature had an important role to play in helping to shape the consciousness of a people lacking adequate literary representation. I listened warily, found myself moved by their radiant youth. When I began to respond I felt aged by caution and skepticism: . . . that I really didn't agree with them. I didn't think that there *was* such a thing as minority literature. Any novel or play about the lower class will necessarily be alien to the culture it portrays. I rambled: . . . the relationship of the novel to the rise of the middle class in eighteenth-century Europe. Then, changing the subject to Alex Haley's *Roots*: That book tells us more about his difference from his illiterate, tribal ancestors than it does about his link to them. More quickly: The child who learns to read about his nonliterate ancestors necessarily separates himself from their way of life. I saw one of my listeners yawn. Another sort of smiled. My voice climbed to hold their attention. I wanted approval; I was afraid of their scorn. But scorn came inevitably. Someone got up while someone else thanked me for my 'valuable time.' The others filed out of the room; their voices turned loud when they got out in the hall. Receded. Left me alone at my desk.

After that I was regarded as comic. I became a 'coconut' – someone brown on the outside, white on the inside. I was the bleached academic – more white than the *anglo* professors. In my classes several students glared at me, clearly seeing in me the person they feared ever becoming. Who was I, after all, but some comic Queequeg, holding close to my breast a reliquary containing the white powder of a dead European civilization? One woman took to calling me, with exaggerated precision, *Miss-ter Road-ree-gas*, her voice hissing scorn. (The students sitting around her seemed unaware of her message.)

Still, during those months, Berkeley faculty members continued to assure me that – they were certain – I would be able to work as a special counselor to minority students. The truth was that I was a successful teacher of white middle-class students. They were the ones who lined up outside my door during office hours, the ones who called me at night. Still, I continued to receive invitations to conferences to discuss the problems of the disadvantaged. Envelopes found their way to my apartment addressed to *Señor* Ricardo Rodriguez. I heard myself introduced at conferences as a 'Chicano intellectual.' (And I stood up.)

4

I remember my minority student years in graduate school and need to remember them also as years of white student protests. I was at Columbia during the student riots of 1968 and later at Berkeley during the Cambodian invasion. Powerful images stay from those days: The rock-shattered window discloses a slow-drifting Vietcong flag against the Greco-Roman facade of the university library; campus policemen with bulbous insectlike helmets are chasing students past the open door of my classroom. It is spring.

With most students and teachers I knew, I was opposed to America's Vietnam War. (For me there were deferments and then, when I was vulnerable to the draft, a high lottery number.) I signed petitions and wrote letters to United States senators. I marched up Fifth Avenue in New York, and I joined demonstrations outside the Oakland Induction Center in California. But I was not a very active participant in that season of protest. I never 'occupied' a school building. Or heaved a rock. I slept soundly through a riotous night at Columbia while students and sirens screamed outside my dormitory window. I walked through picket lines to study in libraries. There seemed to me something sadly unserious about the militancy. Student demonstrations at Berkeley always blossomed when the weather turned fine. Many students who demanded that the university be 'shut down' were careful to check with instructors to be certain they would get course credit at the end of the quarter. Too often the engagement with violence seemed playful. Students rushed to assume, without irony, the role of society's victims.

Victims. At Berkeley, that institution which symbolizes middle-class opportunity, students complained about the impersonal life on the campus – they were being reduced to IBM numbers. But they seemed not to realize that the reason most of them could receive higher education was that universities as vast as Berkeley existed, replacing more private (more exclusionary) institutions of higher learning. White women on campus proclaimed their sisterhood with working-class women. 'We all are oppressed,' they insisted. Then went on to demand the 'solution' of affirmative action, thereby repeating the mistake of claiming benefits for the relative few because of the absence of the many. Students gathered at lunchtime in front of Low Library at Columbia or on Sproul Plaza at Berkeley to hear student radicals claim their union with 'the people.' And nobody laughed.

It was one thing for poorly schooled nonwhite students to claim that they were minorities. It was ludicrous for white middle-class students to claim social oppression. They were not victims. They were among the fortunate ones, America's favored children. They were the ones with the opportunity for higher education. It is true that as more and more persons were graduating from college in the sixties, the diploma's value on the job market diminished. Nevertheless, college students were different from those in America's underclass. Many college graduates were forced to work as cabbies or waitresses after graduation, but they retained the confidence of a public identity. They knew how to survive in institutional America. (Students certainly knew how to deal with their draft boards. It wasn't any coincidence that most of those drafted to fight in Vietnam were working-class teenagers, out of high school.)

I was at Berkeley in 1974 when the romantic sixties came to an end. A more pragmatic time succeeded it. Reporters for *Time* and for CBS informed the nation that a new mood of careerism had seized the campus. ('Suddenly . . .') Suddenly students in my classes admitted to being ambitious for good grades. Freshmen had already mapped the progress that would lead them to business or law school. (Professional schools were the only places which dispensed diplomas promising jobs.) Students would come to my office to challenge the grade of *B* they had received. ('Couldn't you please reconsider, Professor

Rodriguez? I need an *A*-minus for my transcript.') They would sit in the back rows of my classes surreptitiously reading biochemistry textbooks, while I lectured on Spenser or Dickens, insisting that the reader of literature is made mindful of his social position and privilege. In such classrooms, before students who were so anxious and uncertain of their social advancement, the enlarging lessons of the humanities seemed an irrelevance.

I cannot say now whether I was more comfortable on the campus of the sixties or the campus of the seventies. I'm not sure that they were such different places. The two eras were not so much in opposition as they were complementary developments, indicative of a single fact: Students at the new middle-class campus lacked deep appreciation of their social advantages. What had been lost in the postwar expansion of higher education was the sense that higher education implied privilege. Thus, for a few years, students could be lured by a romantic idea of their victimization. And after a few years students could embrace mean careerism. In either case, self-pity was triumphant.

White students in the seventies frequently complained to me about affirmative action. They said that the reason they couldn't get admitted to business school or the reason their fellowship application had been rejected was the minorities. I tried to sympathize with the convenient complaint. I was on record as being opposed to affirmative action. But I was increasingly annoyed by the fact that the white students who complained about affirmative action never bothered to complain that it was unfair to lower-class whites. What solely concerned them was that affirmative action limited *their* chances, *their* plans.

I would tell fellow graduate students about my outrageous

good fortune. Smiling at my irony, I would say that I had been invited to join 'minority leaders' on trips to distant Third World countries. Or I would mention that I had been awarded a thousand dollars for winning an essay contest I had not even entered. Or I would say that I had been offered a teaching job by an English department. Some listeners smiled back, only to say: 'I guess they need their minority.' The comment silenced me. It burned. (It was one thing for me to say such a thing; oddly hard to hear someone else say it.) But it was true, I knew.

In the seventies, as more and more Americans spoke out against affirmative action, university presidents were forced to take the defense. They spoke for the necessity of creating a non-white leadership class. But their argument was challenged by a man named Allan Bakke – a man of the new university, a man ambitious for his future, caught in the furious competition for professional school. He suggested a middle-class hero of a sort as he struggled for success and asserted his rights. I supported his claim. I continued to speak out in opposition to affirmative action. I publicly scorned the university presidents' call for a nonwhite leadership class. This defense seemed to me to belong to an earlier time, before World War II, when higher education could ensure positions of social power and prominence. I did not yearn for that older, more exclusive (less open) type of school. I wanted, however, something more from the new middle-class institution than either the decadent romanticism of the sixties or the careerism of the seventies. I wanted students more aware of their differences from persons less advantaged. I wanted university presidents to encourage students to work to improve the condition of disadvantaged Americans. To work, however, not as leaders but in order that the socially disadvantaged could lead their own lives.

My thoughts on the issue were printed. But by the late seventies the debate over affirmative action concerned itself only with the rights of white middle-class students. Opinions came from both sides. One heard from politicians and social activists and editorial writers. Finally, the justices of the Supreme Court rendered their judgment in the case of *Bakke v. University of California.* (Bakke was admitted to medical school.) But no one wondered if it had ever been possible to make higher education accessible to the genuinely socially disadvantaged.

5

In 1975, I was afraid of the success I knew I would have when I looked for a permanent teaching position. I accepted another one-year appointment at Berkeley in an attempt to postpone the good fortune awaiting me and the consequent issue it would finally force. But soon it came time: September, October, November – the traditional months of academic job-searching arrived. And passed. And I hadn't written to a single English department. When one of my professors happened to learn this, late in November, he was astonished. Then furious. He yelled at me over the phone. Did I think that just because I was a minority, the jobs would come looking for me? Didn't I realize that he and several other faculty members had already written letters on my behalf to various schools? Was I going to start acting like some other minority students he knew? They struggled for academic success and then, when they almost had it made, they chickened out. Was that it? Had I decided to fail?

I didn't want to respond to his questions. I didn't want to admit to him – thus to myself – the reason for my delay. I agreed to write to several schools. I wrote: 'I cannot claim to represent socially disadvantaged Mexican-Americans. The very fact that I am in a position to apply for this job should make that clear.' After two or three days, there were telegrams and phone calls inviting me to job interviews. There followed rapid excitement: a succession of airplane trips; a blur of faces and the murmur of soft questions; and, over somebody's shoulder, the sight of campus buildings shadowing pictures I had seen, years before, when as a scholarship boy I had leafed through Ivy League catalogues with great expectations. At the end of each visit, interviewers would smile and wonder if I had any questions for *them*. I asked if they were concerned about the fact that I hadn't yet finished my dissertation. Oh no, they said. 'We regularly hire junior faculty members who complete their dissertation during their first year or two here.' A few times I risked asking what advantage my race had given me over other applicants. But that was an impossible question for them to answer without embarrassing me. They rushed to assure me that my ethnic identity had given me no more than a foot inside the door, at most a slight edge. 'We just looked at your dossier with extra care, and, frankly, we liked what we saw. There was never any question of our having to alter our standards. You can be certain of that.'

In the first part of January their offers arrived on stiff, elegant stationery. Most schools promised terms appropriate for any new assistant professor of English. A few made matters worse by offering more: an unusually large starting salary; a reduced teaching schedule; free university housing. As their letters gathered on my desk, I delayed my decision. I started calling department chairmen to ask for another week, another ten days – 'more time to reach a decision' – to avoid the decision I would have to make. (One chairman guessed my delay to be a bargaining ploy, so he increased his offer with each of my calls.)

At school, meanwhile, I knew graduate students who hadn't received a single job offer. One student, among the best in the department, did not get so much as a request for his dossier. He and I met outside a classroom one day, and he asked about my prospects. He seemed happy for me. Faculty members beamed at the news. They said they were not surprised. 'After all, not many schools are going to pass up the chance to get a Chicano with a Ph.D. in Renaissance literature.' Friends telephoned, wanting to know which of the offers I was going to take. But I wouldn't make up my mind. Couldn't do it. February came. I was running out of time and excuses. I had to promise a decision by the tenth of the month. The twelfth at the very latest . . .

February 18. The secretaries in the English department kept getting phone calls; there were messages left on yellow slips of paper: Where was I? What had I decided? Have Professor Rodriguez return my call (*collect*) this evening. Please tell Richard Rodriguez that we must have a decision from him immediately because budget estimates for next year are due at the end of the week.

Late afternoon: In the office at Berkeley I shared with several other lecturers and teaching assistants, I was grading some papers. Another graduate student was sitting across the room at his desk. At about five, when I got up to leave, he looked over to tell me in a weary voice that he had some very big news. (Had I heard?) He had decided to accept a position at a faraway state university. It was not the job he especially wanted, he said. But he needed to take it because there hadn't been any other offers. He felt trapped and depressed, since the job would separate him from his young daughter, who would remain in California with her mother.

I tried to encourage him by remarking that he was lucky at least to have found a position. So many others hadn't. . . . But before I finished, I realized that I had said the wrong thing. And I anticipated what he would say next.

'What are your plans?' he wanted to know. 'Is it true that you've gotten an offer from Yale?'

I said that it was. 'Only, I still haven't made up my mind.'

He stared at me as I put on my jacket. And then stretching to yawn, but not yawning, he asked me if I knew that he too had written to Yale. In his case, however, no one had bothered to acknowledge his letter with even a postcard. What did I think of that?

He gave me no chance to reply.

'Damn!' he said, and his chair rasped the floor as he pushed himself back. Suddenly it was to *me* that he was complaining. 'It's just not right, Richard. None of this is fair. You've done some good work, but so have I. I'll bet our records are just about even. But when we go looking for jobs this year, it's a very different story. You're the one who gets all the breaks.'

To evade his criticism, I wanted to side with him. I was about to admit the injustice of affirmative action. But he continued, his voice hard with accusation. 'Oh, it's all very simple this year. You're a Chicano. And I am a Jew. That's really the only difference between us.'

His words stung anger alive. In a voice deceptively calm, I replied that he oversimplified the whole issue. Phrases came quickly: the importance of cultural diversity; new blood; the goal of racial integration. They were all the old arguments I had proposed years before – long since abandoned. After a minute or two, as I heard myself talking, I felt self-disgust.

The job offers I was receiving were indeed unjustified. I knew that. All I was saying amounted to a frantic self-defense. It all was a lie. I tried to find an end to my sentence; my voice faltered to a stop.

'Yeah, yeah, sure,' he said. 'I've heard all that stuff before. Nothing you say, though, really changes the fact that affirmative action is unfair. You can see that, can't you? There isn't any way for me to compete with you. Once there were quotas to keep my parents out of schools like Yale. Now there are quotas to get you in. And the effect on me is the same as it was for them. . . .'

At the edge of hearing, I listened to every word he spoke. But behind my eyes my mind reared – spooked and turning – then broke toward a reckless idea: Leave the university. Leave. Immediately the idea sprang again in my bowels and began to climb. Rent money. I pictured myself having to borrow. Get a job as a waiter somewhere? I had come to depend on the intellectual companionship of students – bright students – to relieve the scholar's loneliness. I remembered the British Museum, a year in the silence. I wanted to teach; I wanted to read; I wanted this life. But I had to protest. How? Disqualify myself from the profession as long as affirmative action continued? Romantic exile? But I had to. Yes. I found the horizon again. It was calm.

The graduate student across the room had stopped talking; he was staring out the window. I said nothing. My decision was final. No, I would say to them all. Finally, simply, no.

I wrote a note to all the chairmen of English departments who had offered me jobs. I left a note for the professor in my own department at Berkeley who was in charge of helping graduate students look for teaching positions. (The contradictions of affirmative action have finally caught up with me. Please remove my name from the list of teaching job applicants.)

I telephoned my mother and father. My mother did not seem to hear exactly what I was trying to tell her. She let the subject pass without comment. (Was I still planning on coming for dinner this Sunday?) My father, however, clearly understood. Silent for a moment, he seemed uncertain of what I expected to hear. Finally, troubled, he said hesitantly, 'I don't know why you feel this way. We have never had any of the chances before.'

We, he said. But he was wrong. It was *he* who had never had any chance before.

SIX

Mr. Secrets

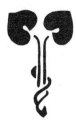

I am writing about those very things my mother has asked me not to reveal. Shortly after I published my first autobiographical essay seven years ago, my mother wrote me a letter pleading with me never again to write about our family life. 'Write about something else in the future. Our family life is private.' And besides: 'Why do you need to tell the *gringos* about how "divided" you feel from the family?'

I sit at my desk now, surrounded by versions of paragraphs and pages of this book, considering that question.

When I decided to compose this intellectual autobiography, a New York editor told me that I would embark on a lonely journey. Over the noise of voices and dishes in an East Side restaurant, he said, 'There will be times when you will think the entire world has forgotten you. Some mornings you will yearn for a phone call or a letter to assure you that you still are connected to the world.' There *have* been mornings when I've dreaded the isolation this writing requires. Mornings spent listless in silence and in fear of confronting the blank sheet of paper. There have been times I've rushed away from my papers to answer the phone; gladly gotten up from my chair, hearing the mailman outside. Times I have been frustrated by the slowness of words, the way even a single paragraph never seemed done.

I had known a writer's loneliness before, working on my dissertation in the British Museum. But that experience did not prepare me for the task of writing these pages where my own life is the subject. Many days I feared I had stopped living by committing myself to remember the past. I feared that my absorption with events in my past amounted to an immature refusal to live in the present. Adulthood seemed consumed by memory. I would tell myself otherwise. I would tell myself that the act of remembering is an act of the present. (In writing this autobiography, I am actually describing the man I have become – the man in the present.)

Times when the money ran out, I left writing for temporary jobs. Once I had a job for over six months. I resumed something like a conventional social life. But then I have turned away, come back to my San Francisco apartment to closet myself in the silence I both need and fear.

I stay away from late-night parties. (To be clearheaded in the morning.) I disconnect my phone for much of the day. I must avoid complex relationships – a troublesome lover or a troubled friend. The person who knows me best scolds me for escaping from life. (*Am* I evading adulthood?) People I know get promotions at jobs. Friends move away. Friends get married. Friends divorce. One friend tells me she is pregnant. Then she has a baby. Then the baby has the formed face of a child. Can walk. Talk. And still I sit at this desk laying my words like jigsaw pieces, a fellow with ladies in housecoats and old men in slippers who watch TV. Neighbors in my apartment house rush off to work about nine. I hear their steps on the stairs. (They will be back at six o'clock.) Somewhere planes are flying. The door slams behind them.

'Why?' My mother's question hangs in the still air of memory.

The loneliness I have felt many mornings, however, has not made me forget that I am engaged in a highly public activity. I sit here in silence writing this small volume of words, and it seems to me the most public thing I ever have done. My mother's letter has served to remind me: I am making my personal life public. Probably I will never try to explain my motives to my mother and father. My mother's question will go unanswered to her face. Like everything else on these pages, my reasons for writing will be revealed instead to public readers I expect never to meet.

I

It is to those whom my mother refers to as the *gringos* that I write. The *gringos*. The expression reminds me that she and my father have not followed their children all the way down the path to full Americanization. They were changed – became more easy in public, less withdrawn and uncertain – by the public success of their children. But something remained unchanged in their lives. With excessive care they continue today to note the difference between private and public life. And their private society remains only their family. No matter how friendly they are in public, no matter how firm their smiles, my parents never forget when they are in public. My mother must use a high-pitched tone of voice when she addresses people who are not relatives. It is a tone of voice I have all my life heard her use away from the house. Coming home from grammar school with new friends, I would hear it, its reminder: My new intimates were strangers to her. Like my sisters and brother, over the years, I've grown used to hearing that voice. Expected to hear it. Though I suspect that voice has played deep in my soul, sounding a lyre, to recall my 'betrayal,' my movement away from our family's intimate past. It is the voice I hear even now when my mother addresses her son- or daughter-in-law. (They remain public people to her.) She speaks to them, sounding the way she does when talking over the fence to a neighbor.

It was, in fact, the lady next door to my parents – a librarian – who first mentioned seeing my essay seven years ago. My mother was embarrassed because she hadn't any idea what the lady was talking about. But she had heard enough to go to a library with my father to find the article. They read what I wrote. And then she wrote her letter.

It is addressed to me in Spanish, but the body of the letter is in English. Almost mechanically she speaks of her pride at the start. ('Your dad and I are very proud of the brilliant manner you have to express yourself.') Then the matter of most concern comes to the fore. 'Your dad and I have only one objection to what you write. You say too much about the family . . . Why do you have to do that? . . . Why do you need to tell the *gringos*? . . . Why do you think we're so separated as a family? Do you really think this, Richard?'

A new paragraph changes the tone. Soft, maternal. Worried for me she adds, 'Do not punish yourself for having to give up our culture in order to "make it" as you say. Think of all the wonderful achievements you have obtained. You should be proud. Learn Spanish better. Practice it with your dad and me. Don't worry so much. Don't get the idea that I am mad at you either.

'Just keep one thing in mind. Writing is one thing, the family is another. I don't want *tus hermanos* hurt by your writings. And what do you think the cousins will say when they read where you talk about how the aunts were maids? Especially I don't want the *gringos* knowing about our private affairs. Why should they? Please give this some thought. Please write about something else in the future. Do me this favor.'

Please.

To the adult I am today, my mother needs to say what she would never have needed to say to her child: the boy who faithfully kept family secrets. When my fourth-grade teacher made

our class write a paper about a typical evening at home, it never
occurred to me actually to do so. 'Describe what you do with
your family,' she told us. And automatically I produced a fic-
tionalized account. I wrote that I had six brothers and sisters;
I described watching my mother get dressed up in a red-sequined
dress before she went with my father to a party; I even related
how the imaginary baby sitter ('a high school student') taught
my brother and sisters and me to make popcorn and how, later,
I fell asleep before my parents returned. The nun who read
what I wrote would have known that what I had written was
completely imagined. But she never said anything about my
contrivance. And I never expected her to either. I never thought
she *really* wanted me to write about my family life. In any case,
I would have been unable to do so.

I was very much the son of parents who regarded the most
innocuous piece of information about the family to be secret.
Although I had, by that time, grown easy in public, I felt that
my family life was strictly private, not to be revealed to unfamiliar ears or eyes. Around the age of ten, I was held by
surprise listening to my best friend tell me one day that he
'hated' his father. In a furious whisper he said that when he
attempted to kiss his father before going to bed, his father had
laughed: 'Don't you think you're getting too old for that sort
of thing, son?' I was intrigued not so much by the incident as
by the fact that the boy would relate it to *me.*

In those years I was exposed to the sliding-glass-door in-
formality of middle-class California family life. Ringing the
doorbell of a friend's house, I would hear someone inside yell
out, 'Come on in, Richie; door's not locked.' And in I would
go to discover my friend's family undisturbed by my presence.
The father was in the kitchen in his underwear. The mother
was in her bathrobe. Voices gathered in familiarity. A parent

scolded a child in front of me; voices quarreled, then laughed; the mother told me something about her son after he had stepped out of the room and she was sure he couldn't overhear; the father would speak to his children and to me in the same tone of voice. I was one of the family, the parents of several good friends would assure me. (Richie.)

My mother sometimes invited my grammar school friends to stay for dinner or even to stay overnight. But my parents never treated such visitors as part of the family, never told them they were. When a school friend ate at our table, my father spoke less than usual. (Stray, distant words.) My mother was careful to use her 'visitor's voice.' Sometimes, listening to her, I would feel annoyed because she wouldn't be more herself. Sometimes I'd feel embarrassed that I couldn't give to a friend at my house what I freely accepted at his.

I remained, nevertheless, my parents' child. At school, in sixth grade, my teacher suggested that I start keeping a diary. ('You should write down your personal experiences and reflections.') But I shied away from the idea. It was the one suggestion that the scholarship boy couldn't follow. I would not have wanted to write about the minor daily events of my life; I would never have been able to write about what most deeply, daily, concerned me during those years: I was growing away from my parents. Even if I could have been certain that no one would find my diary, even if I could have destroyed each page after I had written it, I would have felt uncomfortable writing about my home life. There seemed to me something intrinsically public about written words.

Writing, at any rate, was a skill I didn't regard highly. It was a grammar school skill I acquired with comparative ease. I do not remember struggling to write the way I struggled to learn how to read. The nuns would praise student papers for being neat – the handwritten letters easy for others to read; they promised that my writing style would improve as I read more and more. But that wasn't the reason I became a reader. Reading was for me the key to 'knowledge'; I swallowed facts and dates and names and themes. Writing, by contrast, was an activity I thought of as a kind of report, evidence of learning. I wrote down what I heard teachers say. I wrote down things from my books. I wrote down all I knew when I was examined at the end of the school year. Writing was performed after the fact; it was not the exciting experience of learning itself. In eighth grade I read several hundred books, the titles of which I still can recall. But I cannot remember a single essay I wrote. I only remember that the most frequent kind of essay I wrote was the book report.

In high school there were more 'creative' writing assignments. English teachers assigned the composition of short stories and poems. One sophomore story I wrote was a romance set in the Civil War South. I remember that it earned me a good enough grade, but my teacher suggested with quiet tact that next time I try writing about 'something you know more about – something closer to home.' Home? I wrote a short story about an old man who lived all by himself in a house down the block. That was as close as my writing ever got to my house. Still, I won prizes. When teachers suggested I contribute articles to the school literary magazine, I did so. And when I was asked to join the school newspaper, I said yes. I did not feel any great pride in my writings, however. (My mother was the one who collected my prize-winning essays in a box she kept in her closet.) Though I remember seeing my by-line in print for the first time, and dwelling on the printing press letters with fascination: RICHARD RODRIGUEZ. The letters furnished evidence of a vast public identity writing made possible.

When I was a freshman in college, I began typing all my assignments. My writing speed decreased. Writing became a struggle. In high school I had been able to handwrite ten- and twenty-page papers in little more than an hour – and I never revised what I wrote. A college essay took me several nights to prepare. Suddenly everything I wrote seemed in need of revision. I became a self-conscious writer. A stylist. The change, I suspect, was the result of seeing my words ordered by the even, impersonal, anonymous typewriter print. As arranged by a machine, the words that I typed no longer seemed mine. I was able to see them with a new appreciation for how my reader would see them.

From grammar school to graduate school I could always name my reader. I wrote for my teacher. I could consult him or her before writing, and after. I suppose that I knew other readers could make sense of what I wrote – that, therefore, I addressed a general reader. But I didn't think very much about it. Only toward the end of my schooling and only because political issues pressed upon me did I write, and have published in magazines, essays intended for readers I never expected to meet. Now I am struck by the opportunity. I write today for a reader who exists in my mind only phantasmagorically. Someone with a face erased; someone of no particular race or sex or age or weather. A gray presence. Unknown, unfamiliar. All that I know about him is that he has had a long education and that his society, like mine, is often public (*un gringo*).

2

'What is psychiatry?' my mother asks. She is standing in her kitchen at the ironing board. We have been talking about nothing very important. ('Visiting.') As a result of nothing we have been saying, her question has come. But I am not surprised by it. My mother and father ask me such things. Now that they are retired they seem to think about subjects they never considered before. My father sits for hours in an armchair, wide-eyed. After my mother and I have finished discussing obligatory family news, he will approach me and wonder: When was Christianity introduced to the Asian continent? How does the brain learn things? Where is the Garden of Eden?

Perhaps because they consider me the family academic, my mother and father expect me to know. They do not, in any case, ask my brother and sisters the questions wild curiosity shapes. (That curiosity beats, unbeaten by age.)

Psychiatry? I shrug my shoulders to start with, to tell my mother that it is very hard to explain. I go on to say something about Freud. And analysis. Something about the function of a clinically trained listener. (I study my mother's face as I speak, to see if she follows.) I compare a psychiatrist to a Catholic priest hearing Confession. But the analogy is inexact. My mother can easily speak to a priest in a darkened confessional; can easily make an act of self-revelation using the impersonal formula of ritual contrition: 'Bless me, father, for I have sinned. . . .' It would be altogether different for her to address a psychiatrist in unstructured conversation, revealing those events and feelings that burn close to the heart.

'You mean that people tell a psychiatrist about their personal lives?'

Even as I begin to respond, I realize that she cannot imagine ever doing such a thing. She shakes her head sadly, bending over the ironing board to inspect a shirt with the tip of the iron she holds in her hand. Then she changes the subject. She is talking to me about one of her sisters, my aunt, who is seriously ill. Whatever it is that prompted her question about psychiatry has passed.

I stand there. I continue thinking about what she has asked me – and what she cannot comprehend. My parents seem to me possessed of great dignity. An aristocratic reserve. Like the very rich who live behind tall walls, my mother and father are always mindful of the line separating public from private life. Watching a celebrity talk show on television, they listen for several minutes as a movie star with bright teeth recounts details of his recent divorce. And I see my parents grow impatient. Finally, my mother gets up from her chair. Changing the channel, she says with simple disdain, 'Cheap people.'

My mother and my father are not cheap people. They never are tempted to believe that public life can also be intimate. They remain aloof from the modern temptation that captivates many in America's middle class: the temptation to relieve the anonymity of public life by trying to make it intimate. They do not understand, consequently, what so pleases the television audience listening to a movie star discuss his divorce with bogus private language. My father opens a newspaper to find an article by a politician's wife in which she reveals (actually, renders merely as gossip) intimate details of her marriage. And he looks up from the article to ask me, 'Why does she do this?'

I find his question embarrassing. Although I know that he does not intend to embarrass me, I am forced to think about this book I have been writing. And I realize that my parents will be as puzzled by my act of self-revelation as they are by the movie star's revelations on the talk show. They never will call me cheap for publishing an autobiography. But I can well imagine their faces tightened by incomprehension as they read my words.

(Why does he do this?)

Many mornings at my desk I have been paralyzed by the thought of their faces, their eyes. I imagine their eyes moving slowly across these pages. That image has weakened my resolve. Finally, however, it has not stopped me. Despite the fact that my parents remain even now in my mind a critical, silent chorus, standing together, I continue to write. I do not make my parents' sharp distinction between public and private life. With my mother and father I scorn those who attempt to create an experience of intimacy in public. But unlike my parents, I have come to think that there is a place for the deeply personal in public life. This is what I have learned by trying to write this book: There are things so deeply personal that they can be revealed only to strangers. I believe this. I continue to write.

'What is psychiatry?' my mother asks. And I wish I could tell her. (I wish she could imagine it.) 'There are things that are so personal that they can only be said to someone who is not close. Someone you don't know. A person who is not an intimate friend or a relation. There are things too personal to be shared with intimates.'

She stands at the ironing board, her tone easy because she is speaking to me. (I am her son.) For my mother that which is personal can only be said to a relative – her only intimates. She makes the single exception of confessing her sins to a Catholic priest. Otherwise, she speaks of her personal life only at home. The same is true of my father – though he is silent even with family members. Of those matters too jaggedly personal to reveal to intimates, my parents will never speak. And that seems to me an extraordinary oppression. The unspoken may well up within my mother and cause her to sigh. But beyond that sigh nothing is heard. There is no one she can address. Words never form. Silence remains to repress them. She remains quiet. My father in his chair remains quiet.

I wonder now what my parents' silence contains. What would be their version of the past we once shared? What memories do they carry about me? What were their feelings at many of the moments I recollect on these pages? What did my father – who had dreamed of Australia – think of his children once they forced him to change plans and remain in America? What contrary feelings did he have about our early success? How does he regard the adults his sons and daughters have become? And my mother. At what moments has she hated me? On what occasions has she been embarrassed by me? What does she recall feeling during those difficult, sullen years of my childhood? What would be her version of this book? What are my parents unable to tell me today? What things are too personal? What feelings so unruly they dare not reveal to other intimates? Or even to each other? Or to themselves?

Some people have told me how wonderful it is that I am the first in my family to write a book. I stand on the edge of a long silence. But I do not give voice to my parents by writing about their lives. I distinguish myself from them by writing about the life we once shared. Even when I quote them accurately, I profoundly distort my parents' words. (They were never intended to be read by the public.) So my parents do not truly speak on my pages. I may force their words to stand between quotation marks. With every word, however, I change what was said only to me.

'What is new with you?' My mother looks up from her ironing to ask me. (In recent years she has taken to calling me Mr. Secrets, because I tell her so little about my work in San Francisco – this book she must suspect I am writing.)

Nothing much, I respond.

I write very slowly because I write under the obligation to make myself clear to someone who knows nothing about me. It is a lonely adventure. Each morning I make my way along a nar-

rowing precipice of written words. I hear an echoing voice –
my own resembling another's. Silent! The reader's voice silently
trails every word I put down. I reread my words, and again it
is the reader's voice I hear in my mind, sounding my prose.

When I wrote my first autobiographical essay, it was no
coincidence that, from the first page, I expected to publish what
I wrote. I didn't consciously determine the issue. Somehow I
knew, however, that my words were meant for a public reader.
Only because of that reader did the words come to the page.
The reader became my excuse, my reason for writing.

It had taken me a long time to come to this address. There
are remarkable children who very early are able to write publicly about their personal lives. Some children confide to a diary
those things – like the first shuddering of sexual desire – too
private to tell a parent or brother. The youthful writer addresses
a stranger, the Other, with 'Dear Diary' and tries to give public
expression to what is intensely, privately felt. In so doing, he
attempts to evade the guilt of repression. And the embarrassment of solitary feeling. For by rendering feelings in words
that a stranger can understand – words that belong to the public, this Other – the young diarist no longer need feel all alone
or eccentric. His feelings are capable of public intelligibility.
In turn, the act of revelation helps the writer better understand
his own feelings. Such is the benefit of language: By finding
public words to describe one's feelings, one can describe oneself
to oneself. One names what was previously only darkly felt.

I have come to think of myself as engaged in writing
graffiti. Encouraged by physical isolation to reveal what is most
personal; determined at the same time to have my words seen
by strangers. I have come to understand better why works of
literature – while never intimate, never individually addressed
to the reader – are so often among the most personal statements

we hear in our lives. Writing, I have come to value written words as never before. One can use *spoken* words to reveal one's personal self to strangers. But *written* words heighten the feeling of privacy. They permit the most thorough and careful exploration. (In the silent room, I prey upon that which is most private. Behind the closed door, I am least reticent about giving those memories expression.) The writer is freed from the obligation of finding an auditor in public. (As I use words that someone far from home can understand, I create my listener. I imagine her listening.)

My teachers gave me a great deal more than I knew when they taught me to write public English. I was unable then to use the skill for deeply personal purposes. I insisted upon writing impersonal essays. And I wrote always with a specific reader in mind. Nevertheless, the skill of public writing was gradually developed by the many classroom papers I had to compose. Today I *can* address an anonymous reader. And this seems to me important to say. Somehow the inclination to write about my private life in public is related to the ability to do so. It is not enough to say that my mother and father do not want to write their autobiographies. It needs also to be said that they are unable to write to a public reader. They lack the skill. Though both of them can write in Spanish and English, they write in a hesitant manner. Their syntax is uncertain. Their vocabulary limited. They write well enough to communicate 'news' to relatives in letters. And they can handle written transactions in institutional America. But the man who sits in his chair so many hours, and the woman at the ironing board – 'keeping busy because I don't want to get old' – will never be able to believe that any description of their personal lives could be understood by a stranger far from home.

3

When my mother mentioned seeing my article seven years ago, she *wrote* to me. And I responded to her letter with one of my own. (I wrote: 'I am sorry that my article bothered you . . . I had not meant to hurt . . . I think, however, that education has divided the family . . . That is something which happens in most families, though it is rarely discussed . . . I had meant to praise what I have lost . . . I continue to love you both very much.') I wrote to my mother because it would have been too difficult, too painful to hear her voice on the phone. Too unmanageable a confrontation of voices. The impersonality of the written word made it the easiest means of exchange. The remarkable thing is that nothing has been spoken about this matter by either of us in the years intervening. I know my mother suspects that I continue to write about the family. She knows that I spend months at a time 'writing,' but she does not press me for information. (Mr. Secrets.) She does not protest.

The first time I saw my mother after she had received my letter, she came with my father to lunch. I opened the door to find her smiling slightly. In an instant I tried to gather her mood. (She looked as nervous and shy as I must have seemed.) We embraced. And she said that my father was looking for a place to park the car. She came into my apartment and asked what we were having for lunch. Slowly, our voices reverted to tones we normally sound with each other. (Nothing was said of my article.) I think my mother sensed that afternoon that the person whose essay she saw in a national magazine was a person unfamiliar to her, some Other. The public person – the writer, Richard Rodriguez – would remain distant and untouchable. She never would hear his public voice across a dining room table. And that afternoon she seemed to accept the idea, granted me the right, the freedom so crucial to adulthood, to become a person very different in public from the person I am at home.

Intimates are not always so generous. One close friend calls to tell me she has read an essay of mine. 'All that Spanish angst,' she laughs. 'It's not really you.' Only someone very close would be tempted to say such a thing – only a person who knows who I am. From such an intimate one must sometimes escape to the company of strangers, to the liberation of the city, in order to form new versions of oneself.

In the company of strangers now, I do not reveal the person I am among intimates. My brother and sisters recognize a different person, not the Richard Rodriguez in this book. I hope, when they read this, they will continue to trust the person they have known me to be. But I hope too that, like our mother, they will understand why it is that the voice I sound here I have never sounded to them. All those faraway childhood mornings in Sacramento, walking together to school, we talked but never mentioned a thing about what concerned us so much: the great event of our schooling, the change it forced on our lives. Years passed. Silence grew thicker, less penetrable. We grew older without ever speaking to each other about any of it. Intimacy grooved our voices in familiar notes; familiarity defined the limits of what could be said. Until we became adults. And now we see each other most years at noisy family gatherings where there is no place to stop the conversation, no right moment to turn the heads of listeners, no way to essay this, my voice.

I see them now, my brother and sisters, two or three times every year. We do not live so very far from one another. But as an entire family, we only manage to gather for dinner on

Easter. And Mother's Day. Christmas. It is usually at our parents' house that these dinners are held. Our mother invariably organizes things. Well before anyone else has the chance to make other arrangements, her voice will sound on the phone to remind us of an upcoming gathering.

Lately, I have begun to wonder how the family will gather even three times a year when she is not there with her phone to unite us. For the time being, however, she presides at the table. She – not my father, who sits opposite her – says the Grace before Meals. She busies herself throughout the meal. 'Sit down now,' somebody tells her. But she moves back and forth from the dining room table to the kitchen. Someone needs more food. (What's missing?) Something always is missing from the table. When she is seated, she listens to the conversation. But she seems lonely. (Does she think things would have been different if one of her children had brought home someone who could speak Spanish?) She does not know how or where to join in when her children are talking about Woody Allen movies or real estate tax laws or somebody's yoga class. (Does she remember how we vied with each other to sit beside her in a movie theatre?) Someone remembers at some point to include her in the conversation. Someone asks how many pounds the turkey was this year. She responds in her visitor's voice. And soon the voices ride away. She is left with the silence.

Sitting beside me, as usual, is my younger sister. We gossip. She tells me about her trip last week to Milan; we laugh; we talk about clothes, mutual friends in New York.

Other voices intrude: I hear the voices of my brother and sister and the people who have married into our family. I am the loudest talker. I am the one doing most of the talking. I talk, having learned from hundreds of cocktail parties and dinner parties how to talk with great animation about nothing especially. I sound happy. I talk to everyone about something. And I become shy only when my older sister wonders what I am doing these days. Working in Los Angeles? Or writing again? When will she be able to see something I've published?

I try to change the subject.

'Are you writing a book?'

I notice, out of the corner of my eye, that my mother is nervously piling dishes and then getting up to take them out to the kitchen.

I say yes.

'Well, well, well. Let's see it. Is it going to be a love story? A romance? What's it about?'

She glances down at her thirteen-year-old son, her oldest. 'Tommy reads and reads, just like you used to.'

I look over at him and ask him what sort of books he likes best.

'Everything!' his mother answers with pride.

He smiles. I wonder: Am I watching myself in this boy? In this face where I can scarcely trace a family resemblance? Have I foreseen his past? He lives in a world of Little League and Pop Warner. He has spoken English all his life. His father is of German descent, a fourth-generation American. And he does not go to a Catholic school, but to a public school named after a dead politician. Still, he is someone who reads . . .

'He and I read all the same books,' my sister informs me. And with that remark, my nephew's life slips out of my grasp to imagine.

Dinner progresses. There is dessert. Four cakes. Coffee. The conversation advances with remarkable ease. Talk is cheerful, the way talk is among people who rarely see one another and then are surprised that they have so much to say. Sometimes voices converge from various points around the table. Sometimes voices retreat to separate topics, two or three conversations.

My mother interrupts. She speaks and gets everyone's attention. Some cousin of ours is getting married next month. (Already.) And some other relative is now the mother of a nine-pound baby boy. (Already?) And some relative's son is graduating from college this year. (We haven't seen him since he was five.) And somebody else, an aunt, is retiring from her job in that candy store. And a friend of my mother's from Sacramento – Do we remember her after all these years? – died of cancer just last week. (Already!)

My father remains a witness to the evening. It is difficult to tell what he hears (his hearing is bad) or cannot understand (his English is bad). His face stays impassive, unless he is directly addressed. In which case he smiles and nods, too eagerly, too quickly, at what has been said. (Has he really heard?) When he has finished eating, I notice, he sits back in his chair. And his eyes move from face to face. Sometimes I feel that he is looking at me. I look over to see him, and his eyes dart away the second after I glance.

When Christmas dinner is finished, there are gifts to exchange in the front room. Tradition demands that my brother, the oldest, play master of ceremonies, 'Santa's helper,' handing out presents with a cigar in his hand. It is the chore he has come to assume, making us laugh with his hammy asides. 'This is for Richard,' he says, rattling a box next to his ear, rolling his eyes. 'And this one is for Mama Rodriguez.' (There is the bright snap of a camera.)

Nowadays there is money enough for buying useless and slightly ludicrous gifts for my mother and father. (They will receive an expensive backgammon set. And airplane tickets to places they haven't the energy or the desire to visit. And they will be given a huge silver urn – 'for chilling champagne.')

My mother is not surprised that her children are well-off. Her two daughters are business executives. Her oldest son is a lawyer. She predicted it all long ago. 'Someday,' she used to say when we were young, 'you will all grow up and all be very rich. You'll have lots of money to buy me presents. But I'll be a little old lady. I won't have any teeth or hair. So you'll have to buy me soft food and put a blue wig on my head. And you'll buy me a big fur coat. But you'll only be able to see my eyes.'

Every Christmas now the floor around her is carpeted with red and green wrapping paper. And her feet are wreathed with gifts.

By the time the last gift is unwrapped, everyone seems very tired. The room has become uncomfortably warm. The talk grows listless. ('Does anyone want coffee or more cake?' Somebody groans.) Children are falling asleep. Someone gets up to leave, prompting others to leave. ('We have to get up early tomorrow.')

'Another Christmas,' my mother says. She says that same thing every year, so we all smile to hear it again.

Children are bundled up for the fast walk to the car. My mother stands by the door calling good-bye. She stands with a coat over her shoulders, looking into the dark where expensive foreign cars idle sharply. She seems, all of a sudden, very small. She looks worried.

'Don't come out, it's too cold,' somebody shouts at her or at my father, who steps out onto the porch. I watch my younger sister in a shiny mink jacket bend slightly to kiss my mother before she rushes down the front steps. My mother stands waving toward no one in particular. She seems sad to me. How sad?

Why? (Sad that we all are going home? Sad that it was not quite, can never be, the Christmas one remembers having had once?) I am tempted to ask her quietly if there is anything wrong. (But these are questions of paradise, Mama.)

My brother drives away.

'Daddy shouldn't be outside,' my mother says. 'Here, take this jacket out to him.'

She steps into the warmth of the entrance hall and hands me the coat she has been wearing over her shoulders.

I take it to my father and place it on him. In that instant I feel the thinness of his arms. He turns. He asks if I am going home now too. It is, I realize, the only thing he has said to me all evening.

ACKNOWLEDGMENTS

Portions of this book were published in earlier, often far different, versions by *The Columbia Forum* (1973); *The American Scholar* (1974); *Politicks and Other Human Interests* (1977); *College English* (1978); *Change* (1978); *The State of the Language*, edited by Leonard Michaels and Christopher Ricks, University of California Press (1980); and *The American Scholar* (1980).

In the crucial first year of writing this book, I was helped by a fellowship from the National Endowment for the Humanities.

has been set by Lamb's Printing Company, Clinton, Massachusetts, in Granjon, a type named in compliment to Robert Granjon, type-cutter and printer – in Antwerp, Lyons, Rome, Paris – active from 1525 to 1590. The boldest and most original designer of his time, he was one of the first to practice the trade of type-founder apart from that of printer.

This type face was designed by George W. Jones, who based his drawings upon a type used by Claude Garamond (1510-1560) in his beautiful French books, and more closely resembles Garamond's own than do any of the various modern types that bear his name.

HUNGER OF MEMORY has been designed by Ann Schroeder and printed on Warren's #60 Antique, an entirely acid-free paper. Haddon Craftsmen, Scranton, Pennsylvania was the printer and binder.